SOULMATE

YOUR ARE MY PRIORITY NOT MY OPTION

SADHU HARSHA VARDHAN

ISBN 979-888503893-5

YOU ARE NOT AN OPTION . YOU ARE MY ONLY PRIORITY

Contents

Contents

Foreword

DEDICATED TO THE BEST

Preface

This story is a love story of Karan Oberoi and Anjali Malhotra. Karan Oberoi is the CEO of Oberoi group of companies and every girl's dream guy. Inspite of having everything, he still feels his life is incomplete. Even though he has a loving and caring people in his life, his past holds him back. Dr.Anjali Malhotra, a doctor by profession. She is beautiful and talented pediatrician who has a natural aura around her that attracts people towards her. Circumstances and family brings them together to get married. Will their marriage bring them closer to each other? Can their forced arranged marriage bloom love in their relationship? To know more, join the journey of Karan and Anjali and see how their survive in their relationship with lots of twist and turn.

Acknowledgements

HOPE YOU LOVE AND ENJOY THE BOOK

Prologue

At the Cafe Dreamplace, a guy in his early thirties was waiting impatiently for a girl. Patience was a not a part of his nature. After drinking a cup of cold coffee and waiting for around half an hour when he decided to hell with this meeting, the person for whom he was waiting this long entered through the front door of the Cafe.

As Anjali entered the busy Cafe, the rich aroma of coffee hit her nostrils. She approached the side table near the window where Karan was waiting for her and sat in front of him.

Ignoring the scwol on Karan's face, first she called the waiter and ordered a cup of cappuccino for herself and then faced Karan with a forced smile.

"Is this your punctuality Miss.Malhotra. If you have not turned up in two more minutes, I would have left the Cafe. I cancelled my important meeting to meet you and you didn't even bothered to come on time." Karan said to Anjali in an angry tone.

"Hello Mister, don't you dare lecture me on punctuality. A new case came at the hospital when I was leaving and since no other pediatrician was available at that moment, I couldn't let a small child be untreated." Anjali replied to him in an equally annoyed tone. She felt that Karan is an arrogant devil since she met him the first time.

"Well let's not waste more time and come straight to the point for which you called me here."Anjali said. "Direct talk and no formalities Miss.Malhotra. I am impressed but believe me even I don't have an extra minute to spend for you." Said Karan with a smirk.

"Arrogant jerk" Anjali muttered under her breath.

CHAPTER ONE

It was a bright sunny day. The sunlight coming from the window lighted the room. As the sunrays fell on the sleeping figure, he shouted to the servants to close the curtains.

"Shyam close the curtains" mumbled Karan sleepily. Hearing his sleepy voice, his mother Anuradha Oberoi chuckled and went near his bed and sat on the side of the bed. She loving started caressing her son's hair and asked him to wake up. But instead of waking up Karan snuggled into his mother's lap. Anuradha gazed at her handsome son while continuing to caress his hair and a flick of sadness crossed her vision.

She wondered when her son will again get his life partner who will take care of him like his late wife Vidhya. She wanted Karan to forget Vidhya and move on in his life as she is not going to come again in his life. Vidhya was not only Karan's love but also the soul of the Oberoi family.

The entire Oberoi family was very happy with Karan's choice when he introduced Vidhya. She was a jolly person who was liked by all and became the loving daughter-in-law to Karan's parents and a caring sister-in-law to his younger sister Pakhi.

But Vidhya's tragic death affected everyone most importantly Karan. He still cannot forget his late wife and their unborn child. Instead of living with a free spirit, he became a hard person.

Anuradha and her husband Sanjay Oberoi prayed to God everyday to send some one like Vidhya again in their son's life. He cannot spend his entire life living like a hollow person from inside. She wish to see her son's life colourful again.

"In which thoughts are you lost Mom? Is everything alright?" Asked Karan as he got up.
"Nothing son was just wondering how you used to always sleep in my lap when you were a child. Even now this habit of yours is not changed."

"What can I do in that, I like to sleep in you lap Mom" said Karan smilingly.
" I will take a shower and join you guys for breakfast" Karan said while going into the bathroom.

"Sure honey, we will be waiting for you" replied Anuradha and then she stood up from his bed and went to join her husband and daughter in the dining room.

After taking the shower, Karan came out of the bathroom with a towel hanging around his waist and went into his walk-in-closet opposite to his bathroom. Opening the closet and searching for a shirt to wear his gaze fell on a blue shirt and a memory of Vidhya instantly came in his mind. Blue is his favourite colour and that blue shirt was her last gift to him before her death.

Keeping the blue shirt at the bottom rack, he picked up the first Armani suit from his wardrobe and wore it. There isn't a moment or thing in his life which doesn't remind him of his late wife. He misses her very much everyday. After dressing, he wore his Rolex watch and combed his hair.

Looking at his own reflection mirror, Karan chuckled sadly that every girl would drool at his mere sight but no one knew that below this handsome man was a hollow person. Sighing he took his wallet, handkerchief, cellphone and his office bag and went downstairs into the living room.

CHAPTER TWO

On reaching the dinning room, Karan spotted his father and sister chitchatting with each other. He admired the bond of his father and sister and wished to have the same bond with his baby girl but she died with her mother even before coming in this world.

Keeping negative thoughts aside, he sat on the table and said to his father " Good morning Dad. What's with this chitchatting early in the morning." His Dad smiled at him and said teasingly "nothing son,your sister just asked me to sign her college report."

At this Karan looked with amusement at Pakhi and said"You again got less mark lil sis?" Hearing this Pakhi glared at her brother and said" I am not lil anymore Bhai. I will be graduating college this year and you still think me as your lil sis only!! And the answer to your question is that I was sick last month and so I couldn't prepare my assignment properly so got less mark but at least I passed OK! Don't you dare tell Mom about this or she will cancel my picnic tour next week."

"What are you asking your brother to not tell me Pakhi?" Anuradha said while taking her seat next to her husband and asked the maids to serve their breakfast."Nothing my dear Mom, I was just asking Bhai to not ask you to give a list of do's and don'ts for my picnic tour" replied Pakhi nervously and added "right Bhai!"

Karan faked an innocence and replied "is that so sis?" Hearing this Pakhi gave a horrified look to Karan and exclaimed with a little high tone "Bhai!!!!!!"

Sanjay laughed seeing Pakhi and Karan's battering and asked both the children to start their breakfast. After breakfast Karan asked his father "Dad will you be attending annual board meeting today in evening?"

Hearing this before Sanjay could reply, Anuradha told Karan "Son today your Dad and me are going to meet an old family friend in the evening so he won't be attending the meeting.... Right Sanjay?" Sanjay looked at his wife and nodded. Karan couldn't help but saw the knowing look passed between his parents and wondered what they both were up to now. Last time when they both had shared this look, they had set up a blind date for him.

So he decided to ask his parents further regarding this "Which family friend are you visiting?" But his mother just randomly named some people and told that he doesn't know them as they shifted to Delhi a few years ago and met recently in a social party.

He glanced at his watch and got up hurriedly from his chair and gathered his belongings as he was already late for the office. He walked towards the front door of their mansion and waved a goodbye to his parents and sister before leaving.

CHAPTER THREE

As I was about to go and have a shower after a tiresome day at hospital, my Mom knocked on my bedroom door and then came in my room carrying a green colour dress with golden embroidery on it and handed it to me.

"Baby doll wear this dress after you freshen up and come downstairs. We are having guests tonight at dinner" said Anita Malhotra to her loving daughter Anjali. "Whose coming at our house Mumma for dinner? And what's with this sudden dinner plan! You didn't tell me about it in the morning!" Anjali asked this to her mother with a little surprised expression.

Her mother replied "One of our old family friends Mr. and Mrs. Oberoi are coming over. Your Dad and me met them recently in one of the social party and invited them for dinner and today morning you were in a hurry to leave for hospital so I couldn't tell you. Now if your questions are over, get shower and dressed. Oberoi's will be coming in an hour."

Anjali nodded to her mother and asked about her dad to which she replied that he is on his way to home. Leave it to her Mom to welcome the guests in their home. She will go crazy looking after the arrangements a day before. Smiling at this, she went to her bathroom and took a relaxing shower. After that she blow dried her hair and went to wear the dress her mother had left for her. Seeing the dress Anjali thought why her mother was asking her to wear such heavy dress if it's just a casual family dinner but knowing her mother's habit of making her look like her princess, she wore the dress and went to her dressing table to wear the matching jewellery.

As Anjali was naturally beautiful with a long brown hair up to waist length cut in style, hazel brown eyes, heart shaped face, cute button nose, petal shaped pink luscious lips and fair skin, she doesn't need to wear any make up. She doesn't like to cake up her face with make up so just applied eye liner and lip gloss and kept her hair open with a small diamond clip at the side of her hair.

Smiling at her own reflection she was ready to meet the guests and went to the living room of their penthouse. Seeing her father Raman Malhotra, Anjali went smiling in her dad's direction and hugged him tight " Good evening Papa. I missed you."

Raman laughed at this and looked at his daughter with adoration in his eyes and returned her embrace " We just met in the morning princess but even I missed you too my doll. How was your day at work?" "Oh Papa don't ask, I performed three surgeries today. It was one hell of a busy day" replied Anjali.

After separating from the hug, Raman looked at his daughter and saw that she was dressed beautifully. He couldn't help but admired his daughter. She was the only child and apple of Raman's eye and light of Anita's life. For her parents, she was the princess and had raised her like one. Inspite of being the only child and daughter of one of the well renowed wealthy lawyer, Anjali was down to earth person. She was good to kind people but if one messes with her then she won't spare them.

"You both father and daughter can talk later. Our guests will be coming at any time now so you better hurry up to freshen up and change Raman" said Anita to her husband as she too got ready and came out from their room. "Yes madam" exclaimed Raman and winked at her before going in their bedroom.

Anita blushed at this and then looked at her daughter. She was in awe seeing her daughter looking so beautiful in her dress "You look lovely baby doll." To this Anjali replied " Thanks Mom and you too look beautiful in this peacock colour saree and yes I didn't see Papa winking at you and you blushing at him."

Anita sequeled at this and was about to reply when Raman came out getting ready and even the door bell rang indicating the arrival of their guests.

CHAPTER FOUR

Anita asked their maid to open the door. Seeing Mr. Sanjay Oberoi and Mrs. Anuradha Oberoi, Anita and Raman stood to hug them and greet them. After her parents greeted their guests, Anjali too greeted Sanjay and Anuradha with a polite smile and bend down to touch their feet.

Both Sanjay and Anuradha were impressed seeing Anjali. According to them, she was not only beautiful in looks but inspite of being a doctor and daughter of rich parents, she was polite and humble.

Raman asked to Sanjay "so Sanjay how is your business going on?" To which he replied "Oh the business is running real smooth, thanks to my son for that. He is the current CEO and handling all our companies." Raman further added to the conversation "Yes Karan is considered as shark in coporate field. I heard he even got the Best Businessman Award last year." Sanjay proudly nodded his head at this.

"So how are all at home Anuradha?" Anita asked Anuradha to which she replied "Daddyji had cardiac arrest last year and died. Karan is as usual busy with his office work and Pakhi is in last year of fashion designing." Hearing about the demise of Sanjay's father, Anita and Raman expressed their condolences and then talked further regarding both business and family. Anjali was sitting besides her mother.

Seeing her sitting silently, Anuradha asked her "Your parents told us you are a doctor dear. Which hospital you work?" Anjali smiled at her and replied "Yes aunty I am a pediatrician and I work in Miracle Hospital."

This time Sanjay asked further "From where you done your medicine course beta?". She replied "From Mumbai Uncle."

Sanjay smiled hearing her and said "Even my son Karan did his Engineering from IIT Mumbai."7

"Madam food is ready" said their maid. So Anita and Raman led them to their dinning room and they all ate their dinner happily while catting. After the dinner, Raman and Sanjay went to have a drink in his study room while Anita, Anuradha and Anjali went to sit in balcony. Their penthouse had a great view of the city.

CHAPTER FIVE

While returning from the Malhotra house, Anuradha was lost in deep thoughts. Seeing her thinking deeply, Sanjay knew her thoughts. So he closed the window partition of his BMW SUV and asked his wife "What do you think about Anjali dear?"

Hearing his question Anuradha turned her head from car window and smiled a little in her husband's direction. "How do you know I was thinking about Anjali only? I could be thinking some thing else."

Sanjay chuckled at this and raised an eyebrow "After almost thirty years of marriage and you still can bluff me Anuradha. Well I can always tell from your look what thought has crossed your mind. So now tell me."

Anuradha replied "what do you think of Anjali Sanjay?"

Sanjay instantly answered "what's there to think. She is a nice girl. Her parents has raised her well."

"I am asking that do you think Karan will like her too? I mean I liked her and I even think that she would be a good life partner for our son!! Don't you think so?"

"I too like her but are you sure that Anjali and Karan will be perfect for each other? We don't know her choice of perfect life partner and even I don't think Karan is yet ready for any relationship." Sanjay said with a sigh.

"Well there is nothing wrong in trying right and moreover Karan will never be ready for any relationship until and unless we push him. It's high time now for him to leave the past and move on. Vidhya is not coming back again and Karan cannot spend his whole life alone."

Sanjay knew from the determined look on Anuradha's face that she won't stop till her goal is achieved. He just prayed to God to give his son a chance again to find his soulmate.

CHAPTER SIX

Next day when Raman was studying a case in his office, his phone rang. Glancing at the caller ID he smiled and answered " Good morning Sanjay. How are you?"

Sanjay replied cheerfully "yes Raman I am fine. Actually I wanted to talk to you regarding an important matter so are free to talk?"

"Yes Sanjay I was just reading a new case. What you wanted to talk about? Is everything alright?" Raman asked.

Sanjay said "yes Raman, everything is fine. Actually yesterday when me and my wife both visited your penthouse, we were impressed by your daughter. You both have done a fine job in her upbringing.We liked her for our son Karan so have you given a thought regarding her marriage?"

Raman was a bit surprised hearing this but then thought for a while that it's right time for Anjali to think of marriage. She had completed her studies and even have a nice job in a reputed hospital. "Well Sanjay actually we have not thought regarding her marriage until now but I think it's right time and age for her to think about marriage and a life partner. I will talk with Anita and Anjali and will let you know regarding this."

"Sure Raman just let me know about Anjali's opinion regarding this" with this he bid goodbye to Raman and turned to face his wife sitting on the sofa of their living room.

"Raman will talk to Anita and Anjali and will let us know regarding their opinion on this matter. Till then we can even talk to Karan and know what he thinks about this, what's say wife?" Anuradha nodded her head at this and said to her husband "How about we talk to Karan about this in the evening after dinner. I am sure he won't be able to make any excuse of work at that time hearing about marriage." Sanjay agreed to his wife idea.

Anuradha was right. They all sat together every evening after dinner talking about their daily routine so Karan won't be able to dodge this topic.

CHAPTER SEVEN

As soon as Karan reached their mansion, Shyam opened his car's door and then took his belongings. Seeing no one in the house, Karan turned back to Shyam and asked "Where is everyone Shyam?"

"Bhaiya Sir and Madam are sitting in the garden and Pakhi Didi has gone to her friend's birthday party."

Hearing this Karan decided to take a shower first as he was very tired from work and then join his parents in the garden.

He walked towards his room and after a long relaxing bath, he changed into his track and t-shirt and went downstairs to garden.

Anuradha and Sanjay were sitting around a round coffee table when Karan greeted them "Good evening Mom. Evening Dad. What are you both talking?"

His mom and dad looked at him and smiled. Anuradha said "Nothing special son just general talks. Me and your dad were waiting for you to come. Are you hungry beta? Dinner is ready."

"Yes Mom I am very hungry today. Let's eat. Due to new staff recruitment today I skipped my lunch."

They all went to dinning room and had their dinner. Afterwards when all three of them were sitting in the living room watching TV, Karan asked his mother "Mom why Pakhi has not come yet from her friend's party?"

"Actually beta she called that all her friend's have decided to stay at her friend Isha's house for night over so she will be coming back tomorrow morning" his mother replied.

Sanjay who was silently watching TV turned his attention towards Karan and thought that it was perfect time now to talk to him regarding Anjali. So he said "Karan I and your mother wanted to talk to you regarding something."

Karan nodded his head at his dad and asked him to continue. Sanjay further said "You remember yesterday we went to our family friend's house for dinner!!!! There we met their daughter Anjali. She is a pediatrician in Miracle Hospital and is very good looking and sweet girl. So your mother and me were considering her for you. What do you think about this beta?"

Hearing his dad, Karan's suspicion of their excited behavior from yesterday got confirmed. They both had known that their family friend had a daughter and with the dinner excuse, both actually went to see and met their daughter. He should have known about it yesterday only. "Dad you know I don't want to marry again. I am happy the way I am and I don't wish to replace Vidhya's position in my life with anyone."

Anuradha knew it would be difficult to make Karan think about another relationship but she was determined to drag her son from his past. She said to Karan "Son we are not asking you to give Vidhya's position to anyone but just make a little space for another person in your life. We want you to come out of your past beta and move on in your life. Vidhya is not coming back and even she will also want you to find your happiness again. Life is too long and lonely son without a partner in it. Your dad and I are not getting any younger dear and soon Pakhi will also get married and will be going to leave this house."

Seeing Karan silent,she continued talking "Anjali is a perfect girl for you son. She is beautiful, smart, humble, educated and comes from a good family. She will make a good wife to you Karan. We are not forcing you but just think about it Karan. We really want you to settle down and have your own family."

Sanjay too said supporting his wife "Take your time to think son. Even I have asked Anjali's dad Raman to talk to her regarding this and let us know her opinion in this matter. We are not forcing you but please don't ignore this relationship."

Karan knew after hearing his parents request that he cannot just dodge this marriage topic this time. So he just nodded his head and went to his room after wishing his parents goodnight.

Lying in his bed, Karan was thinking about Vidhya. Why she came into his life if she was supposed to leave him alone in their journey of marriage. He wished she was alive so he doesn't need to be with anyone else.

It's been two years since Vidhya and their unborn baby departed from this world but he still misses them specially Vidhya. She was Karan's happiness and reason to live. After she died, he was just living for the sake of his family. He immersed himself in his work too deep so her thoughts didn't cross his mind much. Since last year his parents are making him meet different girls and asking him to marry again but every time he just avoided it.

But it seems that this time he couldn't quite ignore their talk. They both were determined to get him married again and they won't stop pestering him until he gives in. He just wished that Anjali would say no to this relationship.

CHAPTER EIGHT

In the evening when Raman was drinking tea sitting in their penthouse balcony with his wife, he asked Anita "What do you think about Anjali's marriage Anita?" Hearing this Anita was a bit surprised. She asked "why this sudden talk about our daughter's marriage Raman? Did anyone asked you anything regarding this?"

"Actually Sanjay called me today in the morning and he said that he and Anuradha liked our Anjali for their son Karan. So I told him that I will talk to you and Anjali regarding this matter and let him know. But I think that now is the right time and age for us to think about our daughter's future. What do you think?"

After thinking for a while Anita replied to her husband "You are right Raman, it's good time now for Anjali to get married. She got her degree and has a good job in hand."

"What do you think about Karan. Yesterday Sanjay told me about Karan. He lost his wife two years ago in a car accident. Do you think it is wise to consider Karan for our daughter?" Raman asked

Anita replied to him "yes even Anuradha told me and Anjali about the death of her daughter-in-law. It was a tragic thing for their family. Poor Karan lost his wife and their unborn child. But hearing from Anuradha about Karan, he seems mature and responsible person. What's his fault if his wife died in an accident. I think he will make a good match for our daughter."

Raman agreed with his wife "yes I have seen Karan in business magazine. He is good looking and a successful businessman. Let's talk to Anjali regarding this when she gets home."

Anita nodded her head in agreement.

CHAPTER NINE

While having dinner Anjali found it quite strange seeing both her parents oddly quiet. It looked that they both were communicating through their eyes but she couldn't quite figure out exactly.

She couldn't bear this mystery anymore and asked to her mother "Mumma is everything alright. Why are you both awfully quiet today. Did something happen?"

Anita just faked a laugh and said "No dear nothing happened everything is ok. Just eat your dinner." Anjali didn't seem to convince herself but then decided to ignore it and ate her dinner.

After the dinner, her parents asked her to sit with them. Raman asked first "How was your day today sweetheart?" Hearing him Anjali smiled and said "it was very good Papa. Two of my patients got discharged today and they both were perfectly healthy leaving hospital. Seeing the small babies back to being healthy gives me satisfaction."

Anita and Raman both felt proud of their daughter seeing her dedication to her profession. She was truly an angel .

"Anjali do you have any one special in your life baby doll?"Anita asked her in a low tone. Anjali sequeled hearing her mother "Mumma!!!!". " If there is anyone special in my life then I would have told you and Papa about him. But what's with this sudden question?"

Anita looked at her husband and he nodded at her and informed Anjali "Dear one alliance has come for you."

"From whom Dad? You know I have not yet thought about marriage."Anjali said.

"Yes dear we know that but your mother and I think that it's right time for you to consider about getting married and the alliance is from Mr.Oberoi. He and his wife think you as good match for their son Karan. You know about Karan first wife right?" Raman asked.

Anjali replied "Yes Papa I know about Karan's late wife and it was a very unfortunate thing to happen with him. I have sympathy for him but what can we do. Life and death are not in our hands."

"Yes baby you are right. We cannot decide how much can we live. It's all Almighty's will. Do you have any objections with this proposal beta. Your father and me think that it's good if you consider this alliance. Karan is a mature and responsible person. I am sure he will keep you happy." Her mother said.

Seeing her parents liking to this alliance, Anjali decided to consider it once and see what happens. She told her father "Papa if you and Mumma think that this proposal is good for me then I don't have any objections. I have already met Sanjay Uncle and Anuradha Aunty and they both are very good people.I would like to meet Karan once before deciding anything."

Raman and Anita became so happy hearing their daughter's opinion and decided to soon arrange a meeting of her with Karan.

CHAPTER TEN

Next day when Karan was having dinner, his father asked him "Son we are going to Malhotra house tomorrow so cancel your meetings for evening." Karan frowned hearing his father. He asked Sanjay "Dad what's so hurry to visit Malhotra family. New employee recruitment is going on in all our companies so I am busy for this whole week. We can visit them any day next week."

By postponing the meeting tomorrow, he can think of some excuse to object this proposal. But his mother insisted saying "Karan recruitment process for all our companies are conducted by our HR team and you are the CEO. Surely your half day absence can be managed by your staff members. We are going to Malhotra house tomorrow and that's final."

When Karan again objected his mother, Sanjay too insisted "yes son your Mom is right. Our staff members are efficient and reliable. I already gave my word to Raman when he called me this morning and invited us all to their home. Even Anjali wishes to meet you once."

Karan sighed "Fine Mom and Dad, I will finish my work by lunch time and will be back from office early tomorrow. Now if you will excuse me, I have some pending work. Goodnight." Wishing his mom and dad goodnight, he went in the study room.

Even when he was trying to read a file for signing a contract with a new company tomorrow, he couldn't concentrate. His thoughts were on tomorrow's visit at Malhotra house. He really not wanted to visit them and he had no interest in meeting Anjali but his parents were not taking no for an answer. Finally after his futile efforts to work, he went to sleep.

Mumma stop fussing over the arrangements. No Prime Minister is visiting our home." Anjali told to Anita who was busy instructing the maid regarding the dinner and arranging the living room properly.

Anita frowned hearing her daughter "Anjali you go and get ready. Oberoi's will be coming soon and wear the new dress I purchased for you yesterday." Saying so she went to their room to check whether her husband got ready or not.

Anjali just shook her head at her mother's craziness and went to her bedroom to get ready. After wearing the new dress her mother bought for her yesterday, she stood in front of her dressing table. Anjali was really impressed by her mother's choice. She looked beautiful in the baby pink dress. Deciding to wear her Ruby pendent set her parents gifted her for her last birthday, she wore a silver Swarovski watch with the jewellery and curled her hair a little.

"Anjali didi come outside, the guests have arrived" the maid said softly from outside. "Ok Seema you go, I am coming." Having a final look in the mirror and taking a deep breath, she opened her bedroom door and went outside to meet her supposed prospective.

Karan was awestruck seeing the beautiful girl dressed in pink clothes looking like an angel descending from Heaven. He had not expected Anjali to look this beautiful. Even Vidhya whom he considered very beautiful didn't hold a candle in front of Anjali. Realizing his thoughts, he frowned at himself that why was he comparing Anjali with his Vidhya. Even though see is more beautiful than her, Anjali still cannot replace Vidhya.2

"Hello Uncle and Aunty. How are you?" Anjali asked Sanjay and Anuradha with a soft smile. "We are fine beta. How are you and how is work going on at the hospital?" Anuradha inquired cheerfully. Sanjay too smiled looking at Anjali thinking that their choice for Karan is right.

Pakhi who was silent till now butted in between "Hey Anjali di, I am Pakhi. My Mother and Father's only daughter." Everyone laughed at her antics and emerged in an easy conversation. Pakhi sat near Anjali as she was bored hearing adults boring general talks and thought to talk with Anjali since she seemed nice to her "you are very beautiful Di."

Anjali smiled at her and said " Thanks dear you too are very beautiful. What are studying Pakhi?" Pakhi laughed and replied "oh Di I am no such genius doctor or engineer like you and my big bro. I like to design so I am pursuing fashion designing."

"We are no such genius Pakhi and you too got talent in designing. I personally believe one should always do what he or she is passionate about."

Anita interrupted Anjali and Pakhi's chitchat and told her "Anjali why don't you show Karan our house." Anjali nodded at her mother and stood up. Seeing her looking at him, Karan too stood up and went with her. On her way to her bedroom, she first showed him her parents room and then took him to show her room "This is my bedroom"

Looking around, Karan liked her taste. It was not girly like pink or purple "Your room has nice beige and coffee colour combination unlike my sister whose room is all pink." Anjali smiled hearing him and said "Even my room in our former house was all pink and orange but now I prefer neutral colors."

Without further beating around the bush, Karan told her directly "As you will be knowing about my late wife, I really can't give you the same feelings that I have for her. My parents insisted to meet you so I couldn't deny them." Saying so he went out of her room.

Anjali was shocked at his behavior. How dare he just says his point and leave her room without even glancing at her. She thought he is a devil in disguise. He was no gentleman as her parents had said about him. Realizing the time, she composed herself and went into the living room to join her family.

Seeing her, Raman asked "where were you dear. We all were waiting for you after Karan came from your room." She took a deep breath and answered her father "Papa actually I just got a call from hospital so it took a bit of time."

Their maid came in the mean while and announced that the dinner is ready. Everyone went towards the dinning room. Anjali was sitting next to Pakhi and opposite Karan. They both just avoided each other during dinner and after budding goodbye to Oberoi's, she was in no mood to talk to her parents regarding Karan. So just made an excuse of headache and went to her room.

CHAPTER TWELVE

Next day Anjali had just completed taking round and checking her indoor patients. The intern who was assisting her said her in a low voice "Mam are you ok? You seem gloomy today." Anjali's mood was not ok since meeting Karan yesterday. He was not what she had expected him. He seemed arrogant, rude and impatient to her.

Signing, she said "yes Garima, I am fine just tired. I slept late yesterday night so am just feeling lethargic. If you don't mind, will you order a cup of coffee for me till then I will go and discharge one of my patients" to which Garima nodded and left to order her coffee.

While drinking coffee in her own cabin, she was thinking what to answer her parents about Karan. She avoided their questions yesterday night and today morning but now she doubted that she wouldn't be able to ignore them anymore. By telling them about the things Karan said to her, she didn't won't to tarnish the friendship between both their parents. Her parents and Karan's parents met each other after a long time. She didn't want to create a rift between their rekindled relationship.

Frustrated she glanced at her watch and saw that it was time for her to go home. Tired she put her belongings in her handbag and went towards her car.

During dinner, she was eating silently when her father asked her "Dear why are not taking anything your food is almost finished from your plate. Aren't you feeling well?"

Anjali don't know how to tell her parents what she was feeling from inside. Instead she said "no Papa I am fine. Just tired from hospital work."

Anita who was waiting to talk to her since morning asked "Anjali beta, what did you and Karan talked yesterday. Did you like him?"

Anjali got uncomfortable hearing her mother. She was trying to avoid this topic since yesterday but now she was confused regarding what to tell her parents. She saw expected look on both their faces. Taking deep breath she replied "it was just formal talks Mamma."

Her father asked "Do you like him dear? Your mother and I liked him very much. You both even look good together. Isn't Anita?" Anita nodded excitedly at this.

"Papa I have not thought about him so just give me some time to think. I don't won't to take any decision in hurry which I will regret in future." Anjali told her parents. Raman and Anita didn't push the matter further and wished her goodnight and went to their room after dinner.

CHAPTER THIRTEEN

Karan was working in his study room when he heard a knock on the door. Hearing come in, Pakhi slowly came inside the study room and sat on the chair opposite to Karan.

Seeing her, Karan asked "why are you not sleeping till now Pakhi. Tomorrow morning you have to get up early, you are going for a college picnic"

"Yes Bhai, I know but I slept late in the afternoon so not feeling sleepy. If I watch TV and mom came to know then she will cancel my trip so I couldn't take that risk and I saw the lights were on in study room so thought why not talk with you for some time." Pakhi said cheerfully. Karan chuckled hearing her and said "what you want to talk about lil sis?"

Pakhi inquired "Bhai did you like Anjali di? I really liked her. She seemed so nice to me."
Karan frowned hearing her. He didn't want to think about Anjali. Not that she was not good. Infact he liked her not only in looks but even her nature. She seem to be a good person. But she deserved someone better than him. He was hollow from inside so what will he be able to give her after marriage.

Pakhi clicked her fingers in front of him and teased "ohh Bhai you became lost in her thoughts just by hearing her name. I will surely tell this to Mom and Dad tomorrow morning. I really wish to hear the good news when I come back from my picnic.

"Pakhi wait it's not what you think" but she was gone from the study room before he could say anything further. Getting frustrated, he too got up and went to his room to sleep but sleep was far away from him. His parents and sister liked Anjali very much and they were ready to do anything to make him agree to marry her.1

In the morning, Pakhi had left for her picnic and Sanjay, Anuradha and Karan were having breakfast. Anuradha started the conversation excitedly "Pakhi told me you liked Anjali son. Is it true? I am so happy. Finally you won't be lonely anymore." Karan was shocked hearing this. Leave it to his family to listen only what they want to hear "Mom I didn't say that I like Anjali."

Sanjay frowned hearing him and asked "so you don't like Anjali?" Karan instantly replied "no Dad it's not that. She seems to be a nice girl."

Anuradha again became excited hearing him "That means you like her. Ohh son you made our day. I will just call Anita and tell her this. I just hope even Anjali agrees to this alliance." Saying so she hopped from her chair and went in her room to call Anita.

Karan got panicked seeing his mother so he looked at his father and requested him "Dad please ask Mom not to call Anita aunty. I don't want to rush things."

His father smiled at him and said "Don't over think son. Some times we just know when things are right. See you in evening. Even I am going to call Raman regarding this. Ohh my son, I am so excited. Finally some will come in your life to drag your ass from work." Chuckling at his own statement, Sanjay too stood up and went to his room.1

Seeing his parents, Karan knew they will say yes to this alliance from his side even without asking him further.

Explaining them anything will fall on deaf ears. Signing he went to his office.

Anjali just entered her home when her mother engulfed her in a bear hug "ohh baby doll, I am so happy today. Anuradha called this morning and told that Karan agreed for this proposal." Anjali gasped hearing this. How come he agree if he clearly told her that he was not happy with this alliance. Some thing didn't seem to be right according to her.

Karan was shouting on his secretary for the missing file when his best friend Arjun entered "hey Bro, wassup?" Karan frowned seeing him and asked his secretary to find the missing file in half an hour. As soon as his secretary left his cabin, he turned towards his friend and glared at him "Why you came in my office at this time and what do you want? I am busy right now so come later." Arjun just laughed hearing this. He and Karan were best friends since their schooling and he knew Karan more than his family so he didn't feel bad at his rude behavior. He was used to his friends mood swings "what happened Karan that got you so uptight?" Asked Arjun.

Karan sighed and told him the entire story about him and Anjali. After hearing everything, Arjun looked at him bewildered and asked "Are you nuts Karan? How can tell any girl that you are not interested in any relationship with her and you are just meeting her for your family's sake only. If I were on her place, I would have kicked you out of my place then and there."

Karan glared at him "I didn't tell you everything so you can taunt me. My parents have gone mad and they called her house and told them that I agreed to this alliance without asking me. If you can't help me then you know the way out."

Arjun sighed and said " it's been two years Karan. Please move on in your life. Everyone needs a partner in our life. We cannot live alone." Karan didn't want to hear this talk again so he said "Arjun I am not interested to hear this talk any further so if you have any idea how to cancel this alliance then suggest me or else I will think of some thing."

Arjun knew it's useless to explain Karan so he told him "Why don't you call Anjali and ask her to meet you somewhere outside without your boths family's knowledge. This way you can apologize to her for your earlier behavior and ask her to say no to this proposal as your parents won't listen to you."

Karan thought for a while at this and he liked his friend's suggestion.

After Arjun left his office, he called Miracle Hospital and asked for Anjali's number. Anjali was busy in checking her indoor patients when her phone vibrated in her labcoat.

She saw the unknown number and wondered who would be calling her at this time. She picked up her phone and replied "Hello Dr. Anjali Malhotra speaking"

"Anjali Karan here. Are you free to talk?" Anjali was shocked hearing him calling her "what do you want Karan. I am busy" she replied a little arrogantly. When he couldn't show any Courtesy in her home then why will she show the same now.

Karan got annoyed hearing her "I want to discuss something important with you so can you meet me today?"

Anjali got confused at this and asked "what you want to talk about?"2

Karan replied "I will tell you that in person just tell me when are you free. I will let you know the time and place to meet."

Frustrated Anjali told him the time when she will be free from work and asked him to text the time and address where to meet.

CHAPTER FOURTEEN

Anjali was thinking about her today's meeting with Karan in the cafe. How dare he tell her to say no to this alliance. If he is having problem then why can't he say no to this. Not that she was eager to agree for this relationship but is she says no then her parents will be upset with her. They are too willing and convincing her to agree to marry Karan.

If she says no then she has to give a valid reason to her parents and she can't tell them what Karan had said her.

Her thoughts were disturbed when she heard a knock on her door. Her mother came in and sat next to her on her bed.

Anita caressed her hair and asked "Are you not feeling sleepy baby doll?" Anjali nodded at her mother and kept he head in her lap.

Anita smiled "you know sweetie, it's hard in today's time to trust a stranger with your life but believe me dear. You won't regret if you will marry Karan. He is a very responsible person. He may not be expressive like other boys of his age but you too understand his point of view. Losing your life partner is not an easy thing. He may take his time in opening up but I know you will give him time and space for it. Your father and I have known Sanjay and Anuradha since you kids were small. They are very trustworthy people. We really wish you to agree for this proposal. Even if we would not be in this world then also we would be happy thinking you are in safe hands."

Anjali got up from her mother's lap and hugged her "Mamma don't say things like that. You and Papa are never leaving me alone ok?"

Anita gave her a smile and said "Anjali dear we are not going anywhere leaving you child but we really wish to see you having your own family. Your father and I have never asked you anything but please beta it's our request to you to agree for marrying Karan. We are your parents and we know what is best for you. Please beta please say yes. You won't appreciate our decision right now but you will thank us one day for this."1

Her mother was right. Anita and Raman have never asked her for anything in her entire life. They had always treated her like a princess they call her. Can't she agree to this proposal for her parents sake.

Thinking this she drifted into a dreamless sleep after her mother went from her room. In the morning when she was leaving for work, she spotted her parents in the living room and went to tell them her decision.

"Papa, Mamma I want to talk to you. I have decided to marry Karan. You both talk with Sanjay Uncle and Anuradha Aunty and tell them my decision." Anjali said to her parents. Hearing their daughter's decision, Anita hugged her tight and said "Thank you baby. You made us so happy today. I will call Anuradha today itself and ask her for Karan's horoscope for setting your engagement and wedding dates." After Anita, Raman kissed his daughter's forhead and asked her "you are happy with this decision right sweetie?" Anjali nodded at her father and hugged him.

She could live with Karan's aloofness entire life but she do not have a heart to refuse her parents wish. If marrying Karan will make her parents satisfied then so be it.

Karan was working in his office when his cellphone vibrated. His mother was calling him "Yes Mom what happened? I am busy right now." Anuradha ignored his working attitude and said "Son Anita called just now and said Anjali agreed for this marriage. I am so happy Karan. Come home early this evening. Anita has called Panditiji at her house so we are going to Malhotra house to set your engagement and wedding dates."

Karan got angry hearing his mother. He specifically asked Anjali to say no to this marriage but here she said yes. Now he had no other way to cancel this marriage. He would have a word with her very soon. "Hello Karan you there son?"Anuradha inquired.

"Yes Mom I am hearing. I won't be able to come today at Malhotra house. I am meeting a client today evening for signing a contract. You people go." He said to his mother. Anuradha frowned hearing her son "Karan it won't look nice if you won't come son. They will soon be becoming a part of our family."

Karan didn't want to go there so he just told his mother that he would join them next time as he cannot cancel the meeting at the last moment. Hesitantly Anuradha agreed and disconnected the call.

After talking to his mother, Karan called Anjali. Seeing Karan calling her, Anjali knew why he was calling her. Sighing she picked up her phone "Yes Karan why you called?"

Karan angrily replied "You have the nerve to ask that when I specifically told you to say no to this marriage. Why you agreed to marry me Anjali? You know I don't want to marry anyone."

Anjali too became angry hearing his accusations "Even I am not dying to marry you. I tried to deny marrying you but my parents were hell bent on convincing me to marry you. I tried ok."

"Then try harder and say no" Karan snapped at her.

This made her more mad and she too replied irritatingly "I tried but couldn't do that so if you have any problem with this marriage then say no to your parents." Saying this she disconnected the call.

She was seething in anger when her mother called her and asked her to come home early as Karan's family is coming to set the dates. But she was in a no mood to meet them today after talking to Karan so she made work excuse and told her mother that she will be late from hospital.

CHAPTER FIFTEEN

Anita, Pakhi and Anuradha were discussing the dates with Panditiji while Raman and Sanjay were deciding the preparations for the wedding. Both Karan and Anjali had given work excuse and were not present.

Panditiji had given the auspicious dates for next month. Karan and Anjali's engagement and wedding dates were decided for next month by their families.

Days went and the preparations was going on for their wedding. Karan and Anjali have not met or talked on phone with each other again after that day.

From tomorrow onwards all the functions were starting. Tomorrow was engagement, next day was haldi in morning followed by sangeet and mehendi in evening. After that on third day was Ganesh Pooja in the morning and wedding in the evening. On fourth day there was reception in the evening.

Anjali was busy packing her bags. Anuradha was sending her drive to pick up Anjali's luggage tomorrow morning. She heard a knock on her door. On opening,she saw her parents and asked "What happened Papa?"

Raman and Anita entered in their daughter's room and said "nothing princess from tomorrow onwards the wedding ceremonies will be starting so all the guests will come and we won't get time to sit and talk. We will miss you sweetie" Raman said getting a little emotional. She had not stayed away from her parents till now. She wondered how will she survive without them.

Seeing tears in Anjali and Raman's eyes, Anita decided to cheer them up. She didn't want her daughter to get upset. Anjali was starting her new life from tomorrow so she wanted her last days in this house filled with joy and laughter. So she said "Princess don't be upset. I will ask Karan to send you to stay with us for few days every month."

Raman and Anjali both laughed at her and all three hugged and sat talking with each other and packing her luggage till late night.

CHAPTER SIXTEEN

WEDDING PART 1

Malhotra house and Oberoi Mansion were both filled with their guests. It was Karan and Anjali's engagement today. Anjali was getting ready in her room when her mother came into her room with the hair stylish "Anjali you hair stylist came. Are you girls done with the make up?" Anita asked Anjali and her cousins who were doing make up on her face.

"Yes aunty Anjali Didi's make up is done."
"Ok girls make her wear her lehenga and jewellery after her hair is done and then bring her downstairs in party hall as soon as she is ready. Guests will be arriving in a few minutes." Anita told the girls and went downstairs to welcome the guests.

Karan was sitting on the stage dressed in Royal blue sherwani and looking around the guests in the party hall when his eyes landed on the stairs. Anjali was coming down the stairs dressed in matching Royal blue and golden lehenga. His breath became rapid seeing her. She was looking drop dead gorgeous. His eyes were glued to her until she came and sat besides him on the stage.

Panditiji started the engagement ceremony by chanting the holy mantras and then asked both of them to make each other wear their rings. Anuradha forwarded the ring to Karan and he put it on her ring finger. Then Anita forwarded the ring to Anjali and she put it on Karan's ring finger. Afterwards the family members and guests came to wish the couple.

Next day, it was haldi ceremony in the morning. Anjali was made to sit in the center of the stage on a low stool wearing a yellow saree and floral jewellery. Her parents, friends and relatives applied turmeric paste to her. Similarly Karan was dressed in yellow kurta and his family, friends and relatives applied haldi to him.

WEDDING PART 2

In the evening,it was Karan and Anjali's sangeet ceremony along with mehendi. Anjali was dressed in orange and pink Indo Western dress whereas Karan was dressed in Peach and white kurta. Anjali's hands and feet were adorned with heena. She saw a small K written in the heart shaped design at the side of her hand and a flick of sadness came in her. She looked at the guests and smiled sadly. People were singing and dancing. The night ended with the blast.

Next day morning was Ganesh Pooja. After that in the evening was the wedding. Anjali was dressed in red and green lehenga with heavy matching antique jewellery. Her cousins were giving a final touch at her look when her parents came into her room.

Anita and Raman both became emotional seeing their daughter's dressed in bridal attire. She was looking like a royal queen. So elegant and beautiful.

"Finally the day came when our house's pride will become someone else's pride. Always remember that we are here for you my darling. We will miss you so much." Anita said with tears in her eyes.

Few tears even slipped from Anjali's eyes. She hugged her mother and said "I will too miss you and Papa." Raman kept a hand on her head and told her "Princess always be happy in your life and love your new family like you love us. Remember if you face any difficulty in your life, we are always there to help you."

As the time for welcoming the groom and family came, Anita and Raman left Anjali in her room to have a final touch up at her look and asked the girls to bring her to Mandap after that.

Again seeing Anjali in bridal attire, Karan was awestruck. She looked divine as a bride.

Soon the priest started chanting the holy mantras and asked the bride and groom to do pheras. After the pheras, Karan was asked to tie the holy chain, mangalsutra, around Anjali's neck and then fill her partition with Vermillion. After a teary goodbye, Anjali went with Karan in his car towards Oberoi Mansion.

There she was welcomed by Anuradha with an aarti and by pushing down the rice pot.

After few small ceremonies and receiving congratulations, Pakhi took Anjali to Karan's room and helped her in changing

CHAPTER EIGHTEEN

After Pakhi helped her to remove the jewellery and free her hair from the hairpins, Anjali didn't wait for Karan. She took her changing bag and went to take a shower. Seeing the see through nighty in her changing bag, Anjali got horrified. Her mother had left a thin piece of silk and lace to wear. She cannot wear that in front of Karan. Even though he was her husband now, she was not comfortable wearing it. Even she didn't want Karan to think of her as desperate.

She peeped from bathroom door and saw that Karan has not yet arrived so wrapping a towel around her body she went out to get her PJs from her other bag. Karan entered his room when Anjali was searching for her PJs in her bag. He looked shocked seeing her wrapped in a towel only. He cleared his throat to make her aware of his presence.

Hearing someone clearing the throat, Anjali turned and looked to see Karan standing awkwardly. He was looking here and there in the room. Flustered she took the first pajama she got from bag and fled to washroom to change.

When Anjali came out of the washroom after getting dressed in her pajama, Karan went in bathroom to take a shower and change. She was wandering around the room in her thoughts. What if Karan expects to have wedding night with her? No that won't happen. He unwilling married her so he too won't force her for anything. Her train of thoughts were broken by clicking of bathroom door. Karan came out freshly showered. He was wearing his t-shirt and shorts.

Anjali was wondering what to talk as they both have not spoken single word to each other since their relationship got fixed.

Finally Karan broke the silence and spoke "My bed is big so we can keep pillows in between and sleep. Couch is very small, your back will be sprained in morning if you will sleep on it entire night."3

With this, he put the extra pillows in the middle of the bed, switched his side lamp and slept. Anjali knew that their marriage won't be any sort of lovey dovey but now that both are married at least they can be decent enough to be civil and polite towards each other. How will their marriage survive if they won't communicate with each other.

Sighing she went to her side of the bed and slept. Sleep was far asleep from both. Anjali was thinking whether they would be able to continue living in this loveless marriage for a long time or not whereas Karan was thinking that even though he was now married to Anjali, how will he be able to accept her as his wife. He cannot give Vidhya's position to anyone else.

CHAPTER NINETEEN

Morning rays fell on Anjali's eyes. She yawned and glanced at the clock on her side table. Seeing the time, she wake up with a jerk. It was 8:30 in the morning and she was still not ready. What will her in laws think of her. It's her first day in her new house. She went into the washroom and took a quick shower and came out wearing shirt and blouse. She thought as Karan was fast asleep, she would quickly wear the saree and get ready.1

Karan was sleeping when few droplets of water fell on his face. He sleepily opened his eyes and saw Anjali drying her hair. He instantly became alert and gulped seeing her creamy white waist. She was wearing a maroon colored saree and her mangalsutra was hanging around her neck. After drying and combing the hair, she filled her partition with Vermillion. When she turned, he closed his eyes and pretended to be sleeping. After hearing the closing of the door, he opened his eyes again and sat on his bed.

How can he be gawking at Anjali Everytime when he still loves Vidhya. Even though she was his wife, she was not Vidhya. Frustrated he went to take a shower and get ready.

When Anjali went downstairs, she saw her mother-in-law and father-in-law sitting in the living room. She went there and bowed down to touch their feet and wished them both good morning.

Her in laws both greeted her with a cheerful smile. "Did you slept well dear? I hope you didn't had any difficulty in your new house." Anuradha asked her gently. Anjali smiled at her mother in-law and replied "yes Mom I slept well. Where is Pakhi? She is not visible yet."

At this Sanjay laughed at her and said "Pakhi is still sleeping beta. You got a lazy sister in-law." Anjali chuckled and said "Don't worry Dad she will learn everything when her time will come. Till then let her enjoy her life."

"Mom what shall I make for breakfast today. It's my first day in this house so what sweet shall I make?" Anjali asked Anuradha. Anuradha got impressed hearing her and replied politely "Make anything you are comfortable with dear. But if you want to know then we three have sweet tooth. Me, Pakhi and your dad eats all the types of sweet but your husband is choosy in sweets. He only like carrot halwa, kheer and gulab jamun. So make any one of these and no need to cook from tomorrow beta. We have cook who prepares our daily meals everyday." Anjali smiled and nodded at her and went to kitchen to make kheer and aloo paratha for breakfast. She liked her in laws. They both so pleasant person. Even Pakhi was very nice to her. Only their son was arrogant but she didn't want to think of this and spoil her day.

Anjali was cooking when Karan came downstairs for breakfast in his business suit. Seeing their son in his office attire, Sanjay asked Karan "Are you going to office Karan?" Karan nodded and answered "Yes dad I am meeting a Japanese client today so I will be back in three hours." Anuradha scowled at Karan and said "Drop Anjali to her parents house for pagphera and have lunch with her family and then bring her home."

Karan got irritated hearing this and was about to object when his father told him "Yes Karan your mom is right. Drop her to her parents house and bring her back with you. This way you will get some time to spend with your in-laws too."

Soon Anjali came along with the food from kitchen. Karan didn't know that Anjali had prepared breakfast. After taking a bite of aloo paratha and kheer, he told their cook "Debu food is really tasty today." Debu smiled and replied him "Baba bhabhiji has made breakfast today. I have just assisting her in the kitchen. So tell her not me."

Karan hesitantly looked at Anjali and said "Food is good Anjali". On this Anjali smiled a little and said him thank you.

CHAPTER TWENTY

Karan was driving his car and Anjali was looking outside the window of the passenger seat. He glanced at her and said "I will be back by lunch time. After taking lunch, we will leave for our home." Anjali just nodded at him and again turned her head to look out of window.

Karan again spoke and said her "We both know the truth of our marriage. You are free to do as you wish. No need to get my opinion or permission for anything. Same applies for me as well. Just pretend to be a happy couple in front of our families." Anjali just gave him a dirty look and looked forward to the road. She didn't find it shocking to hear such words from Karan but it still hurts. Even though he cannot love her, he can still show to be caring. She was his wife and his responsibility now.1

As soon as the car stopped in front of her parents building, she got out from it and went inside the building without giving a single glance at Karan. Karan just sighed at her behavior and started his car to go towards his meeting venue. In the way, he was not feeling well. Even though he asked Anjali to not expect anything from him, he is her husband now. He cannot just ignore his responsibility towards her.

After the meeting, Arjun who was eyeing Karan right from the time meeting started realised something was wrong. He went and sat in the chair next to him and asked "what happened bro? You look lost today." Karan shook his head and replied "I am fine Arjun. Stop irritating me."

"Now it's confirmed that you are upset regarding something. Tell me. May be I can help you" Arjun asked. Karan sighed and told him "I don't know what to do anymore Arjun. I asked Anjali to mind her own business and not expect anything from me but instead of fighting, she just ignored me like I don't exist for her. I want to accept this marriage but I feel that by doing this I am deceiving Vidhya. But then seeing dullness on Anjali's face and knowing that it is because of me, makes me feel guilty. I am really confused. I don't know what to do anymore."1

Arjun who was listening to Karan intently answered "Karan it's just been a day you got married. Just give some time to your relationship and stop comparing Anjali with Vidhya. You need to leave your past buddy. Vidhya too asked you to find your happiness again before she closed her eyes. Somethings are not in our hands bro. We cannot fight fate. Anjali is your present and future. Please try to know her better and give this relationship a chance. For the past, why are you spoiling your present and future Karan. Make peace with it and stop torturing yourself and your family."

Karan just nodded at Arjun and left to go to Anjali's home.

Anjali was sitting with her parents. Seeing her dull face, Anita inquired "Anjali what happened? You seem to be in deep thoughts since you arrived dear? Did anyone said anything to you?" Anjali didn't want her parents to worry about her. She replied "No Mumma no one said anything to me. Infact dad, mom and Pakhi are very nice people. It's just that I am tired. Due to sleeping on a new bed, I couldn't get much sleep." Anita and Raman both sighed in relief and all three continued with their talks.2

Doorbell rang and Anjali instantly became alert. She knew it would be Karan. She just wished he behave normally so her parents won't be able to feel the tension between them. The maid opened the door and Karan came into the living room where all three were sitting. "Good afternoon Mumma, Papa. How are you both?" Karan asked bowing down to touch their feet. Anita and Raman both greeted him with enthusiasm. Then he looked at Anjali and gave her a small smile. Anjali sighed in relief and smiled back.

"Are you hungry son? Lunch is ready. We were just waiting for you. Anjali told you were having a meeting with an important foreign delegate." Raman asked. Karan nodded and replied "Yes Papa meeting was scheduled one month earlier and the client was leaving back for his country this evening so I couldn't cancel it. Let's have lunch. I am hungry."

After the lunch, Karan sat and talked with his in-laws for a while and after that he and Anjali both left for Oberoi Mansion.Anjali was silent throughout the ride and went inside the house as soon as Karan stopped his car without waiting for him. He knew she was angry at him but this is childish behavior. Angrily he too went inside after parking his car in garage.

CHAPTER TWENTY-ONE

Pakhi saw Anjali entering the house "Bhabhi you came. I was waiting for you. Where is Bhai?" Anjali smiled at her and said "Your brother is parking the car. Why were you waiting for me dear. Do you need anything?"

"No Bhabhi I don't need anything. Just some of my friends have came to meet you so let's go to my room." She told cheerfully. Anjali went with Pakhi to her room whereas Karan went straight to their bedroom. After the dinner, Karan was lying in their bed and reading a business magazine when Anjali came inside. She took her nightdress and went into the washroom. After taking a shower and changing, she came out of the bathroom and was applying her night cream when she saw Karan looking at her from the mirror. She averted her eyes and went to sleep with her back to him. Karan saw that she was still not talking to him. He thought it was enough and asked her "Why are you avoiding me?" Anjali said without turning back " I am not avoiding you. Just trying not to interfere in your life. You made it very clear that our relationship is namesake only so I am just following you."

"Damn it Anjali! I asked you not to expect anything from me. I didn't asked you not to talk to me or ignore me. You are making it obvious for others too." Karan snapped at her. Anjali wake up and sat on the bed scwoling. She glared at Karan and told him "what you expect from me Karan? Even I was also not ready to get married yet. Still I agreed for my parents. I too wished for a married life filled with love and happiness. I didn't get it but then I am still trying for our families. I accepted you with your past and what you did. I know you still love your first wife but I was hoping that we can at least be friends. But you are busy giving me cold shoulder and even today morning you made it clear to me to mind my own business."

Karan felt guilty hearing her "I am sorry for my behavior. It's just that I am really confused. I don't know what to do. I cannot give you Vidhya's position in my life." Anjali understood his point of view and said "I know Karan that you still love Vidhya and I am too not taking her place in your life. But can't you give me a little space in your life? Even I am trying hard Karan. Please let be friends instead of living like a stranger."

She knew that it's hard for Karan to leave his past but she was his wife now. Vidhya is no more and now it was her responsibility to look after Karan. She decided to make him come out of his shell and help him in moving forward in his life. She extended her hand towards him and asked " So Mr. Oberoi friends?" Karan thought for a while and then smiled and took her hand "Friends Mrs.Oberoi." Anjali's heart skipped a beat hearing her new name from Karan. They both talked for a while and slept with a smile on their faces. Anjali hoped tomorrow will bring new rays of light in their life.

CHAPTER TWENTY-TWO

Next day Anjali was helping their cook in making breakfast when Anuradha came in the kitchen. "Good morning beta. What are you doing in kitchen?" Anuradha asked Anjali. Anjali smiled at her and said "nothing mom was just helping Debubhaiya in preparing breakfast." Anuradha nodded at this and asked her to wake up Karan as breakfast will be ready in some time.

Anjali went upstairs in their bedroom and stood for a few minutes wondering how to wake up Karan. Finally she said softly " Karan wake up. Breakfast is ready and everyone is waiting for you." Karan didn't budge at this. After few futile attempts, she shook him by his shoulder. Karan lazily told her "let me sleep for some time more Vidhya"

Anjali stiffened hearing this and stood straight. Pakhi entered their bedroom and frowned seeing Karan still sleeping "Bhabhi why have you not woken up Bhai yet. Mom and dad are waiting for you both downstairs for breakfast." Anjali stammered "Actually.. I tried.. " Pakhi went near the bed and shook Karan hardly "Bhai wake up." Karan woke up with a jerk and glared at Pakhi "Is this the way to wake up anyone Pakhi?" Pakhi just shrugged her shoulders and said "it's the only way you wake up Bhai. Poor bhabhi was waking you up from last half an hour. God Bhai you sleep like a log. Now get ready and come downstairs. Mom and dad are waiting for breakfast." Saying this she went out of their room.

Karan looked at Anjali "Good morning. Sorry you were waking me up but I am actually a bit lazy to wake up in morning" he said scratching his neck. Anjali just nodded at him and asked him to take a shower and come downstairs and went out. Karan frowned at her and thought everything was alright between them the night before so what happened now? Suddenly he remembered that someone was waking him up and he told Vidhya not to wake him. "Ohh freak!!" He exclaimed loudly. How can he be so stupid. Yesterday he just settled things with Anjali and today he addressed her as Vidhya. No wonder she behaved stiffly with him. He quickly went in bathroom to take and shower and join his family for breakfast. He thought to talk to Anjali and apologize to her.

CHAPTER TWENTY-THREE

"Good morning everyone. Sorry I am a bit late for breakfast" Karan greeted his family as he sat besides Anjali. Sanjay teased him " no need to say sorry son as you are always late for breakfast."

Karan smirked and asked his mother "Oh really dad! Mom didn't I got this habit from dad?" Anuradha scwoled at Sanjay and said " it's your mistake Sanjay. He learned that from you. Now eat Karan, breakfast is getting cold. Serve him Anjali beta." Anjali put the breakfast in a plate and passed it to Karan without looking at him. Then she poured a cup of tea and passed it to him but still didn't look at him. Karan who was watching her intently sighed. He need to talk to her after the breakfast.

His mother went to Temple and his father went to meet his friends at his club. Pakhi went to college so he thought it's appropriate time to talk to Anjali and apologize. He saw her going to garden and went after her. "Do you like flowers?" Karan asked from behind. Anjali was picking up flowers to put in the vase. She just nodded at him and continued doing her work. He sighed and said "Anjali I am sorry. I didn't mean to address you as Vidhya intentionally. It's just that she use to wake me up by shaking my shoulder. I know we both agreed to leave the past behind and have a fresh start in our relationship and the next day only I started my day by remembering my past. Sorry."

Anjali finally turned around and kept the flowers on the nearby bench "How many times you will say sorry Karan? Just try to remember that I am your wife now not Vidhya. I know it will take time but please try to take the efforts." Karan nodded and asked her "Mom, dad and Pakhi will be home in evening so have you planned to do anything?"

Anjali replied " No I was just thinking of taking a nap after lunch. What about you? Are you going to office?" Karan shook his head and said " no I will go to office on Monday now. I was just wondering if we could go for a lunch if you wish." Anjali became excited at this and nodded cheerfully. "Ok then go and get ready. I need to buy few shirts so first we will go to the mall and then we can go to have our lunch." He said to her. Anjali quicky went to her room to get ready and came out wearing blue knee length dress. "I am ready" Anjali shouted enthusiastically. Karan in awe seeing her in this dress. They both went towards his car and drove off to the mall.

CHAPTER TWENTY-FOUR

After shopping, Karan asked Anjali "what you want to eat Anjali?" Anjali thought for a while and said "I am in a mood to eat Italian so if you too like it, we can have it for lunch." Karan took her to an Italian restaurant nearby the mall and after having lunch, they both drove back to home. Anuradha and Sanjay were sitting in the garden having their tea when Karan and Anjali came holding shopping bags.

The elder couple became happy seeing them going out together. "Good evening Mom, dad!" Anjali sequeled and hugged Anuradha from behind. Anuradha kept her hand on her and asked "Good evening dear. You both went for shopping?" Karan smiled at her and nodded his head. Anjali told them " I will just keep the everyone's bag in their room and come. After she went Sanjay told Karan "I have booked tickets for both of you for Bora-bora. Our private jet is gone for maintenance so you will be flying commercial this time. Your both will be leaving tomorrow for your honeymoon and will stay there for one week. The hotel reservation is done" Karan gasped hearing his father and objected "you should ask once dad before booking tickets and hotel. I have lots of pending work so please cancel the tickets." Anuradha and Sanjay knew Karan won't agree for it so she said "Karan your dad confirmed your work schedule from your secretary yesterday. There is no such work which requires your immediate attention and don't worry, your dad will look after office work in your absence. Even Anjali have one more week leave before joining hospital. So just go and spend some quality time together son. You both will be busy with your respective works afterwards. Think this as a vacation." Karan was silent so Sanjay further supported Anuradha and said "yes Karan your mom is right. Take a vacation and get to know each other better. I will look after office. Moreover you both will get to spend time with each other this way. Please son don't say no." Karan knew his parents were right. He too doesn't want anyone to doubt his marriage with Anjali. He just wondered how will his wife react to this. Anjali came and sat in a chair next to her husband and asked "anything new I didn't hear?" Sanjay smiled at her and said "yes dear we were telling Karan that you both will be leaving for your honeymoon tomorrow for one week. You are still on leave for one more week and even Karan doesn't have any important work in office." Anjali frowned hearing this and looked at Karan to which he just shrugged.

After dinner when they were in their room, Anjali asked Karan "why didn't you told Mom and Dad that we don't want to go on honeymoon?" Karan kept his laptop aside and said "I told them to cancel this trip but they both were not agreeing. Moreover why to make it obvious to others that we just got married forcefully. Moreover I have not taken a vacation in a long time so let's just go there and relax." Anjali thought for a while. Karan was right in a way and it will even be better for their relationship. They will get some private time with each other. She said " shall we start with our packaging? I am tired and want to sleep after that. Tomorrow also we have to leave for airport early morning." After that she and Karan packed their luggage and slept.

CHAPTER TWENTY-FIVE

Karan and Anjali reached Bora Bora in the evening. They checked in their beach side villa. Anjali gasped seeing their villa "oh the villa and the view from it is so exquisite Karan" she squeled holding Karan's hand. A jolt of electricity passed through him where she touched. Karan smiled at her and took back his hand. Anjali too became aware of this and excused herself to go to washroom. Afterwards they ordered for room service after both were tired from a long flight and wanted to sleep early.

In the morning as the sunrays entered the room and ocean's sound was coming from window, Anjali stretched her hands to wiggle but she thought someone had trapped her. Her legs were entangled with two big legs and her waist was enclosed by a pair of muscular arms. She turned and saw Karan hugging her and sleeping. She at once removed herself from him and stood up from the bed. How come he slept besides her when they both slept at two ends of the bed yesterday night. Thank God that he was still sleeping she thought. Anjali went into the washroom to take a shower and came out dressed in a pair of skirt and crop top. Karan who was now awake gasped seeing her. How come someone look so beautiful every time he see her, he wondered.

They both went to have their breakfast after he got ready and then went to explore the town. In evening both went to the beach. Anjali was dressed in her swim suit and sitting in their lounge chair reading her book when Karan saw few men eyeing her as a piece of meat. He angrily clenched his fists and thought how dare they look at his wife. He went towards Anjali's chair and sat besides her by keeping an arm around her shoulder. She was surprised seeing this and asked "what are you trying to do Karan?"

Karan was speechless at this. What was he thinking. How come he become possessive for her when he doesn't have any feeling for her. He quickly stood up and excused himself. Anjali was confused at his behavior but then thought to ignore him and continue reading.

Next few days were good for them. They both talked till late nights, went sight seeing and swimming during day time. Finally it was their last day of honeymoon when Karan took Anjali on a surprise dinner on a yatch. Anjali was impressed by his efforts and thought to buy him a surprise gift.

Next evening when they were in airport waiting for their flight, Karan was busy checking his email when she decided to stroll around. While passing through a watch store, she saw a beautiful watch operated by sensing a person's heartbeat. She thought it's perfect for Karan and bought it for him.

CHAPTER TWENTY-SIX

(Mature contents ahead)

Things were going smooth between Karan and Anjali after their trip to Bora-bora. Both slowly started understanding each other and opening up. One day when Karan reached home from the office in the evening, Anjali had still not come from hospital. Maybe some emergency would be there, he thought. After waiting for two hours and calling several times on her phone, she was still not home. Karan was angry at her. She could have informed that she could be late. It was cloudy outside and the weather was due to rain any time. He called his parents to ask about Anjali. They had gone to attend a relative's wedding in Mumbai. Maybe they had talked to her today and knew about her whereabouts. After not getting any proper answer, he called her parents but even they didn't know about her. He then called Pakhi who was staying at her friend's home for a night but she was also not aware regarding this. Karan again called Anjali's cellphone but no response.

Frustrated he took his car keys and went to hospital. It was raining heavily. Karan stopped his car and got out when he spotted Anjali in the parking lot hugging a male of around his age. He clenched his fist and his gaze became hardened. He went near them and cleared his throat. Anjali who was drenched in rain, turned around and saw Karan standing there. She asked surprised "you here Karan?"

Karan glared at her and told "I was waiting for you at home since two to three hours and you were not picking up your phone. I even called our families but they were also not aware about your whereabouts and since it was raining, I thought to come to hospital and check on you but you seem to be busy."

Anjali smiled and said "actually I was in surgery so my phone was on silent and then my car was not starting so Dr. Keval helped. I was just thanking him. Anyways, this is dr.keval. He is the cardiologist here and my friend and Keval he is my husband Karan.

Keval smiled and extended his hand for a handshake "Hi Karan nice to meet you." Karan briefly shook his hand and turned towards his wife "we all are drenched in rain so I think we should go now Anjali otherwise I will catch cold. Leave your car here only. I will drop you tomorrow." Anjali nodded at him and went towards his car.

While driving, she told "you should have not bothered. I would have come home by my own." Karan just ignored her and continued to drive. On reaching home, he straight away went to their room. Anjali was confused regarding what happened. What she did now that made him angry. Sighing she too went to change. Karan was checking his mails went Shyam entered their room carrying food plates. Anjali tried to talk to him during dinner but Karan just answered her in monosyllabic word and continued eating. After dinner, she stood in front of him when he went to sleep. " What I did now Karan? Why are you not talking to me?" She asked irritating.

Karan replied "I am tired Anjali. Let me sleep" Anjali still insisted "no some thing is wrong. Tell me!!" Karan who was controlling himself snapped at her "I was worried sick for you and you didn't even bother to inform if you are late!

Several thoughts were running in my mind. What would I have done if something happened to you. On top of that, you thank a stranger by hugging him standing in the middle of the rain!"

Anjali was shocked at him "He is my friend Karan not a stranger. How dare you doubt me? And my phone was in silent and I forget to check it. I was in a hurry to reach home after the surgery as I was already late. But you just want to get a chance to snap at me."

Karan glared at her and asked "really Anjali do I always intend to find a chance to snap at you?" Anjali didn't replied. He caught her by her waist tightly and again asked "Answer me damn it!" Anjali felt guilty at her accusation and suddenly hugged him tight "I am sorry Karan. I didn't mean to say that. It's just everything was fine between us these few months and then we fight today. I am really sorry." Karan was taken by surprise. He felt an unimaginable peace having Anjali in his arms. Without thinking, his hands automatically tightened around her waist and he hugged her back. No sound were heard in the room except their breathing and the sound of rain outside. Anjali felt warm and secure in Karan's arms. He smelled her hair and when she got out of his hold, she stared in his eyes. Her hands were still around his neck and his hands were still around her waist. They both were lost looking in each other's eyes. Karan felt at peace after a long time. His body was longing for Anjali's touch in a way he couldn't imagine whereas Anjali was feeling butterflies in her stomach. His touch was creating a havoc in her body.

Slowly she brought her lips close to him and kissed him slowly. Karan didn't responses for few seconds but then he pulled her towards him and kissed her back passionately. They both for fighting for dominance. After both parted their lips due to lack of breath, Karan continued kissing her along her jawline, neck, collar bone. Anjali moaned at this and fisted her fingers in his hair.

Karan again kissed her on her lips and slowly lifted her up in his arms and carried her towards their bed without breaking their kiss. He howered over her and started kissing and touching her body. Anjali was lost in his touches. Her body was burning with desire. She moaned which made Karan's desire more intense. He slowly removed both of their clothes and explored every inch of her body throughout the night.

CHAPTER TWENTY-SEVEN

Anjali was sleeping hugging Karan when the alarm vibrated. She carefully got out of his hold and snoozed the alarm and sat on the bed with her head resting at the backside. She lifted the blanket to wear her night gown and covered Karan properly with the blanket who sleeping naked under it. A small smile adorned her lips and pink stained her cheeks thinking of yesterday night. What happened yesterday was not planned by any of them but then it was magical between them. She didn't regret anything happened infact she now knew her true feelings for her husband. The care, possessiveness or sympathy for him was not just her liking. It was her love for Karan. Yes she loved him and yesterday she got to experience it. She didn't know how, when or where but she fell hard for him. He was still arrogant, rude devil but now her devil and she liked him the way he was.

She knew it would be difficult for Karan to reciprocate her feelings. He still loved Vidhya. She just hoped to have a small but special position for her in his heart. She kissed him on his forhead and went to take a shower.Meanwhile Karan opened his eyes when he heard the bathroom door closed. His sleep was disturbed by moving of Anjali's body but he didn't opened his eyes. He didn't know how will he face her now.

Everything happened yesterday was not supposed to happen. How can he couldn't control himself seeing her.

According to him, he not only did wrong but even cheated Vidhya. How come he forget her because of Anjali. She came in his life since few months only whereas Vidhya was in his life since so many years. Karan became angry on himself. The feelings he was having for Anjali was confusing her. He expected to see her everyday when he returned from office. If she is not seen anywhere, his eyes searched only for her. He enjoys talking to her and listening her. He doesn't like anyone seeing or touching her even for a handshake or a friendly hug. Whenever she is not around, her thoughts occupy his mind. Seeing her crying, makes him feel miserable and seeing her laugh, makes his day. He didn't felt such strong feelings for Vidhya. He never felt possessive seeing Vidhya with any of her male college or friends whereas he becomes barbaric caveman seeing Anjali laughing or talking with anyone male except him.

He never felt uneasy for Vidhya whereas he becomes worried sick if Anjali is stuck outside for work. He cannot have such feelings for Anjali. He cannot undo what happened between them but he need to do something real soon. He cannot let Anjali to come close to his heart. He was lost in his thoughts when Anjali came dressed in her work clothes from the washroom.

She saw Karan was lost in deep thoughts so she cleared her throat to catch his attention and greeted him good morning with a pleasant smile. Karan looked at her and gave her a forced smile and went to take a shower. She frowned seeing his aloofness. Did he regret what happened she thought but then she thought that she was being paranoid. He won't touch her if he doesn't feel anything for her. Brushing her thoughts, she got ready and went downstairs for breakfast. Anjali and Pakhi were waiting for Karan to join them for breakfast. Seeing him come downstairs, Pakhi greeted him good morning and asked him to join them when he shook his head negatively and said "I am late for a meeting so you both have your breakfast. I will have it in the office"

Anjali tried to stop him saying "atleast have an apple Karan" but he just went in a hurry from there. Sighing, she eat with Pakhi and left for hospital. In the hospital after checking her patients, she was sitting in her cabin and thought to call Karan. She wanted to hear his voice so she dialled his number but it went straight to his voicemail. She thought maybe he would be busy with his work. After sometime, she went to her home with eagerness to meet Karan. Anjali was greeted by her in-laws when she reached home. " how are you dear?" Sanjay asked seeing her. Anjali replied cheerfully "I am fine dad. How was your and mom's trip? Did you both enjoyed the wedding?" Anuradha saw the happiness reflecting from her. She and Sanjay both shared a knowing look and smiled at each other. She replied to Anjali "yes beta the wedding was beautiful. We enjoyed a lot. Anything new happened in our absence?" she asked purposefully. Anjali blushed hearing her question and said "nothing new mom" Just then Pakhi came from college and hugged her parents. They all four chatted for a while and then she went to freshen up in their room.

"Anjali call Karan and ask him when will he come home? Dinner is ready" Anuradha asked her. She nodded and called Karan but again her call was going straight to voicemail. Just then he entered the living room. Karan saw Anjali as soon he entered the house. She smiled seeing him but he ignored her and greeted his parents "Good evening mom, dad. When you both returned?" Sanjay replied "Just this evening only. Why are you late today son. We all were waiting for you. Go and change and then join us for dinner"

Karan nodded at him and went in his room to change. During dinner, he informed his family "I am going to Australia tomorrow morning to finalise an important deal.don't know when I will be back."

Anuradha frowned hearing this and asked "why are you leaving in hurry Karan?" Karan shrugged and said "actually mom everything got finalised today only so I have to leave tomorrow itself." Everyone nodded at him and continued their dinner but Anjali was feeling as if Karan was lying. She thought to ask him when they go their room.

After the dinner, as soon as Karan and Anjali came in their room, she asked him "why are going to Australia Karan?" Karan frowned hearing her and said "what do you mean why? I told that I have an important work there. now if you excuse me, I will pack my bag" Anjali asked "should I pack your bag?" Karan snapped at her and told "I don't need your help ok. And if you still want to help then please leave me alone." Anjali gasped hearing this and tears welled up in her eyes. "What happened Karan? Why are you angry on me? Did I do something? If so please tell me. I promise I won't do it again" Karan snapped at her hearing this "Didn't you got what you wanted yesterday night Anjali. Now leave me the hell alone woman." Anjali was left speechless hearing this. Whatever happened yesterday was by mutual consent of both of them. Did he really thought that she was just with him because of this. Anger clouded her vision and she told Karan angrily "How dare you accuse me of such thing Karan. Whatever happened between us yesterday was with both our's consent. Why didn't you controlled yourself if you thought it was wrong?

Karan knew he was wrong in blaming her when he was too equally involved in it but still he was blinded by rage and argued "You knew I was not in right senses. you could have stopped me. you know that i still love Vidhya. Let me tell you that if you think that after whatever happened between us, you can take Vidhya's position then you are sadly mistaken. Whatever happened between us was a mistake. I regret it and please try to stay in your limits from now on" Saying this, he angrily marched out of his room. Anjali was dumbstruck hearing him and fell dowm on the floor crying.

CHAPTER TWENTY-EIGHT

Karan took a bottle of whiskey and went in the study room. He opened the bottle cap angrily and started drinking directly from it. He didn't want to accuse Anjali and say her harsh things but damn it! He can't control himself. He needed to get away from her as fast as possible.

Anjali was sitting on her their bed hugging her knees and crying. Her she thought she would confess her feelings for him and what Karan did? Accussed her and made her feel like a cheap characterless women. How can she live with him now when her self-respect was crushed. She tried to drag him from his past but he was not ready to let it go. She cannot do anything more to save their relationship if Karan was not interested. If he wants to get away from her, she too won't force him to stay together. May be they both are good living away from each other. She too can't live with him now after hearing him.

Next day Anjali was sleeping with her head resting on the backside when Karan entered their room. His heart tightened seeing her face dried of tears. he quickly went to get ready and left for airport after saying goodbye to his parents and sister. Due to crying late last night, Anjali woke up late in the morning. Not seeing Karan's luggage, she knew that he must have left. Her head was banging from inside. Groggily she woke up from the bed and went to take a shower. After a long hot bath, she got ready and left to work. Her head and heart were both aching. She couldn't concentrate on her work so she left hospital early and went to her favourite place in the park. Whenever she feels down, she used to come here. She was sitting on a bench seeing children playing. She was hoping that Karan will say good bye to her before leaving but he made it very clear that there was no more hope left in their relationship. What will she tell to her parents if she doesn't want to live with him anymore. Everything in his house reminds her of him. How can she go back there and pretend as if nothing happened. How will she face their families? How can she be so stupid falling for a hollow person like him. She was angry on everyone who brought him in her life. She wanted to go away from all and far from this place where she can't have a reminder of her failed relationship with him. Karan had no right to break her heart like this. Her parents had no right to force her in this loveless marriage. She was sitting and crying thinking this when her cellphone rang.

She looked at the caller ID and wondered who would be calling her from an unknown number. She picked up the call and said "Hello Dr. Anjali Obe.... Ummm Dr. Anjali Malhotra speaking?" "Hey Anjali how are you girlfriend? It's been so long since we talked" came a cheerful voice from other side. Anjali was speechless hearinh her best friend Shreya on the phone. She wanted to ask her so many things but she couldn't bring her voice out. She was hearing her best friend after two long years. "Anjali you there dear?" asked her friend. "Yes I am here only. How dare you called me after two long years Shreya. You know how much I tried to contact you after you left to London suddenly. How can forget me Shreya and leave me alone" she complained crying. "Ohh Anjali believe me dear even I was miserable here without you. I couldn't get over my parent's death even after trying. Then my uncle one day suggested me a job requirement here in London. I instantly applied for it and got selected. I left the next week. I came to your home before leaving but you had gone for a vacation so couldn't meet you. I wanted to make peace with my loss before contacting you again but when I came to know that you got married, I couldn't stop myself and called you. How is married life treating you girlfriend. I can't believe you got married! I am so happy for you dear" she exclaimed happily. Anjali started crying hearing about her marriage. She and Shreya were best friends and they shared everything with each other. she needed someone to pour her heart her so she told her everything about her marriage with Karan right from the start. After hearing everything, Shreya angrily told her "How can you be so foolish Anjali. You did everything in your power to save your relationship and he just stated you as a cheap woman. How dare he? Let me talk to him" 1

Anjali replied "No Shreya no need to talk to him. It's my fault to fall for him. He made it clear right from the start that he cannot accept me as his wife. Our relationship was for namesake only according to him. I shouldn't have expected anything more than friendship from him" Shreya sighed and asked her worriedly "What are you going to do now Anjali? Have you talked with your parents regarding this?" Anjali too thought of this but didn't know what to do "I don't know Shreya what to do anymore. I don't want to tell this to my parents as they have high regards for Karan. I just want to get away from everything and everyone. I am feeling suffocated here. Please take me away from all these" she requested helplessly. "Hey hey don't cry. If you want to get out from there, come here to London. I will arrange everything for you here but will it be wise to come here without informing your family?" Shreya asked to which

Anjali replied "If I will tell bot the families everything, they will try to make Karan and me understand. I know Karan is not interested in this relationship any more and even I too can't live like this. After I leave, Mumma and Papa will hopefully understand my reason. I can't see them living miserably due to me. If I don't have any contact with them, I won't be able to see their helplessness. They will learn to live without me."

Shreya knew that there was no point now in changing her mind. She knew Anjali was stubborn when decided to do something. Moreover with time, she would be able to heal and contact her family again. Sighing she said "Ok since you want to get away without informing anyone, I will book your tickets for London tomorrow. Come here and live me dear. I will help you in starting your new life here" Anjali thanked here and asked her to mail her flight details to her. Then she went home.

CHAPTER TWENTY-NINE

Four years later.....1

Karan was working on his laptop when he heard a knock on his office door. "Come in" he said strictly. He saw his new PI entered his cabin and instantly became alert. It's been four years since his Anjali left him. He still remembered that fateful day when he came back home only to find that his wife has left everyone and went away somewhere. During his stay in Australia, he finally realized that he cannot deny his feelings for her anymore. He loved her. His love for her was much deeper than his love for Vidhya. Without Vidhya, he felt alone but without Anjali, he felt incomplete. She was that missing part of his life without which he was lost. He knew he had hurt her in the most vulnerable way but he would make it up to her. Next day deciding to apologize to her and confess his feelings, he went back to India only to get the biggest shock of his life. After Anjali left, he told both of their families the reason she left. everyone was angry at him but he was determined to gain everyone's forgiveness including Anjali. In these last four years, he regretted and redeemed and gained forgiveness of all his family members. Even his bond with Anjali's parents became very much strong. He visits them daily so they don't feel lonely.1

Since last four years, he is been living with a single goal to find his wife and bring her back to his home where she rightfully belongs. But no PI's till now have found her. It was like she was vanished from the face of the earth. But he was not stopping till he gets the result. He would move back and earth to find her. She was his true soulmate and he won't live without her.

He gestured his PI to sit and asked "Any news of my wife?" The PI smiled and nodded his head. Karan's heart skipped a beat at this. Finally after four year long wait, he would get to know about Anjali. He gestured him to continue. PI forwaded a brown envelop in front of him and said "Sir your wife's information is in this envelop. She is living in London since last four years with her best friend Shreya. She has two kids preferably twins. A boy and a girl of around three years and working in St. Joseph Hospital as senior pediatrician. She is not seem to be involved in any relationship. Overall, I think she lives a simple life in London"4

Karan was shocked hearing about the kids.He calculated the time period of their marriage consummation and knew that the kids were his. He has two kids and Anjali is hiding them from him. How dare she keeps his kids from him, he thought angrily. He asked his PI to leave thanking him for the information. Even though he was angry at Anjali, he knew she had her reasons to keep the twins away from him. He hadn't exactly presented him as ideal husband to her. But he won't waste any more day in his kids life. He had already wasted three years of their life because of his stubbornness but not anymore. He was determined to get his family back at any cost. He stood up from his chair and went home to inform their families about this.

CHAPTER THIRTY

Next day Anjali got ready for work and then joined her in-laws for breakfast. She was leaving day after tomorrow for London and want to spend some time with them. She will miss all three of them. They had welcomed her with open arms since day one. But she was going to miss Karan the most. Seeing her silent, Pakhi teased her "What happened Bhabhi? Missing Karanbhai?" Anjali stiffened hearing his name "No actually I was thinking about a surgery I am performing today. It's quite critical" she replied. Anuradha kept her hand on her and said "Don't worry beta. You are very capable and talented Doctor. You will do well" "Yes dear don't worry. Everything will go well" said Sanjay. She smiled at them and left for hospital after the breakfast.

Karan had not called her or send her a single message since the day he left. As if it was like he was not there in her life at all. Why was she thinking of him when he was clearly not interested in her. Frustrated, she mailed her resignation to the hospital Dean and handed over her patients to other doctors. After that next day she went to meet her parents and spend some time with them. She wanted to engrave every last memory of each member of the family before leaving because she didn't know when will she be able to meet them again.

After spending a day with her parents, she went to her home. That home which she would be leaving forever within 24 hours. Smiling sadly at the irony of life, she packed her luggage and wrote a letter to both the families saying her final good byes and apologizing for leaving without informing. Next day, she woke up early in the morning before anyone notices her leaving. she had booked a cab last night. Taking a last look at the house, she wiped her tears and sat in the cab and drove off to airport.

Shreya had come to pick-up Anjali from the airport. Seeing her coming out, she ran towards her and hugged her tight. Anjali too hugged her and started crying. Seeing her cry, Shreya wiped her tears and said "Hey girlfriend from now onwards you are living in London with this great personality so don't cry. Welcome to your new life. We will be together again like old times and do lots of fun" Anjali gave her a watery smile hearing this and both the friend's drove towards Shreya's home.

"Welcome to my humble home Your Highness" Shreya bowed dramatically and welcomed Anjali in her condo. It was a beautiful condo with a beach view. Anjali looked around the house in wonder and exclaimed "Wow Shree you are having a nice house here. I will be definitely living here with you" Shreya thanked her and took her to the guest room to get freshen up and rest.

Days went by and Anjali slowly got adapted to this new lifestyle and environment. New job, new people, new country but still the pain and longing in her heart didn't reduced. One day when she was checking her patients, she felt dizzy. The nurse who was assisting her made her sit and gave her a glass of water. "Are you feeling well Doctor?I can call Dr. Stephen is you are not feeling ok?" asked nurse Stella worriedly. Anjali told her "No need Stella. I will myself go and consult with her affter my shift overs". After her OPD timing was over, she went to Gynec Department and got herself checked. She was feeling nauseous and dizzy since last few weeks. Even her period was delayed. She thought it was because of stress but she wanted to confirm it.

"Congratulations Anjali you are six week pregnant" Dr. Jennifer informed her enthusiastically. Anjali was shocked hearing this. How come she didn't know that she was pregnant. They had not used protection that night. How can they be careless. Thanking her absentmindedly, she went to her new home. as soon as Anjali entered the condo, Shreya asked her "Where were you Anjali? Why are you late today? I am so hungry so hurry up get changed till then i will reheat the food" Anjali just sat on the sofa with a thud without bothering to reply her. Seeing her blank expression, Shreya rushed to her side and asked holding her hands "What happened Anjali? Is everything ok?" not getting any reply from her she asked with a high tone again "God Anjali you are scarring me now. Tell me what happened" Anjali looked at her with tears in her eyes and said in a meek voice "I am pregnant" Shreya was shocked hearing this. After sometime, she asked "Now that you are pregnant Anjali, what will you do? Have you thought about it?" Anjali sighed and said "I don't know Shreya! I just started my new life and now I am having Karan's baby"

Shreya slowly asked her "Do you want to keep this baby Anjali?" Anjali looked shocked aat her and replied "Of course Shreya, I am keeping the baby. It's not just Karan's baby but mine too. I will nurture this baby with so much love that he won't need anyone in his life. and you too will help me, don't you?" Shreya nodded enthusiastically and said "I will definitely be helping you with this little one. After all I will be his Masi. We will take care of him, don't worry. But now mommy-to-be, you need to take care of yourself and be happy all the time. I will be personally looking to your meals from now own, understood? I don't want my niece/nephew to be born malnourished" Anjali smiled hearing her and nodded her head. Even though, she would miss her family especially Karan in welcoming this little one in this world, she will do everything in her power to give him a good life.

Anjali stretched her arms to switch off the alarm. She yawned and woke up and went to washroom to take as shower. After getting ready, she went into the twins room. Shreya had gotten married and went to live with her husband so now Anjali was living in her condo along with her kids.

She slowly entered their room and opened the curtains. Then she lifted their blankets and kissed both of their cheeks. "Good morning my babies. Time to rise and shine munchkins" she said waking them up. Her baby boy just turned his head in his pillow where as her baby girl lazily opened her eyes and gave a sweet smile to her mother. Anjali lifted her in her lap and cooed her "Come on sweetie wake up darling. It's time for Mommy to go to hospital and you both to your school" She just snuggled into her mommy's neck. Anjali laughed and said "Come on dear open your eyes. You are a good girl right. Let's wake up you brother also and then you both can brush your teeth and mommy will give you two bath. Then we will wear new clothes and go to play school" Hearing new clothes, Kiara instantly opened her eyes and started waking up Aarav. She one by one lifted both the kids and took them to bathroom to get ready.

It's been four years since she left India and three years her starlets came in her life. She often missed her family especially Karan. His thought irritated her. She don't want to spoil her day remembering him. Shreya helped her a lot when twins were born. She was indeed her true friend. Without her, she couldn't imagine what she would have done.

"Mommy tummy hungry" Aarav said sweetly. Anjali smiled at him and asked "What my lovelies want to eat in breakfast?" Both the kids though for a while and shouted "Rainbow pancake"

After eating pancakes, she dropped the twins to their playschool. "Don't do any mischief darlings. Mommy will meet you both in the evening. Aunt Clara will pick up both from school. Please do as she says ok" Aarav and Kiara both nodded at her and she stooped down to their level to kiss their cheeks. They both kissed each of her cheeks in return and went inside the campus waving her bye. Anjali too drove towards the hospital.

CHAPTER THIRTY-TWO

Anjali entered her condo to find pindrop silence. Normally both the kids would be playing and watching TV at this time. She kept her purse on the coffee table and shouted "Where are you babies. I am home" Hearing her their nanny Clara came out from kitchen holding two glasses of milkshake. "Madam both the kids are in their room drawing. I just made milkshake for them" Clara said. Clara gave the glasses of milkshake to Anjali and left saying her goodbye.

Anjali went into the twins room and saw both were arguing. She kept the glasses on the side table and sat with them "Hi babies. Why are you both are arguing with each other?" Kiara complained her "Mommy Aarav scratched my drawing" Anjali raised an eyebrow at Aarav and asked "Why you did that Aarav?" Aarav replied "She was drawing wrong Mommy. Teacher asked to draw a family picture. I draw you, me and Kiara but she draw Daddy too. We don't have Daddy right Mommy" Anjali gasped hearing this. She wanted their kids to have a father but they were too small and innocent to understand their problems.

Kiara asked her "Mommy do we have a Daddy?" Anjali felt tears stinging her eyes. She couldn't speak so just nodded her head at them. Even though, their father was not with them she wanted them to know about him when the right time comes. "Then why Mommy Daddy is not with us?" Aarav asked innocently. Anjali took a deep breath and told them "Daddy is busy working honey so he couldn't come to meet us but he will soon finish his work and come to meet you both ok"

Both the kids got satisfied hearing her and then she made them drink their milkshakes. That night after she tucked the twins in their bed, she was lying on her bed thinking how will she tell the bitter truth of her marriage to both the kids when they grow up. She really hoped that her situation would be different so even her children have a father figure in their lives like others. Thinking this, she drifted to sleep.

Next day after dropping her children to their playschool, she was on her way to the hospital when Shreya was calling her. "Hi Shree!" Anjali asked . Shreya replied "Hi girlfriend how are you and how are my little ones? Due to this new job, I can't even come to meet them these days" Anjali told her "We all are fine how are you and Abhishek?" Shreya replied "We too are good dear. Actually I called to give you a good news. I am pregnant. Just got to know yesterday" Anjali sequeled hearing this "Oh my God Shree I am so happy for you. Congratulations dear. How is your health and baby's?"

"Ohh God relax Anjali. Me and baby both are fine. Abhi is there to take care of us so don't worry. But I am really missing the twins please bring them to meet me. Even Abhishek was missing them too" Shreya requested her to which Anjali agreed and told "Ok you take care I will bring them to your house when I will get time ok. Even I was thinking to meet you and Abhi. It's been long since we last met" After talking for a while, she disconnected the call and went into the hospital.

CHAPTER THIRTY-THREE

Karan spotted her parents at his in-laws house when he went there to give them the news about Anjali. "You here mom and dad. How are you Mumma, Papa?" He addressed all four of them. Raman smiled and asked him to sit with them. "Why are you here at this hour Karan? Is everything alright?" Anita asked worriedly. Karan grinned and told "Yes Mumma everything is fine infact I came to share a good news" All four were surprised seeing Karan this happy after a long time. Anuradha asked "What good news son?" Karan happily told them "I found Anjali" There was perfect silence hearing this. Raman stood up and asked "Where is my baby Karan?" Karan smiled and said "She is living in London Papa and now she is even a mother of twins, a boy and a girl. I am father of two adorable three year old babies" Everyone was shocked at this news. Finding Anjali was a dream come true for them but having grand kids was an added bonus. Sanjay too got up and asked Karan "Karan call our pilot and ask him to get the jet ready. We are leaving for London"

Karan shook his head and said "No dad I will go to London alone. I want to spend some time alone with my family. But you all don't worry. I won't return back without them. I made a mistake once but won't repeat that again."

Everyone agreed with Karan. Soon enough his jet was in air flying to London. He was sitting in his seat when he called his PI "Mail me the details of my wife and children's daily schedule."

It was night time in London when his jet landed there. He decided to go to his hotel and get rest as he was hell tired wrapping up his work on a short notice. Tomorrow morning he will meet his wife after four long years and his children for the first time. Will they will accept him as their father and how will Anjali react seeing him? Whatever the consequence will be, he will get his family back.

Next day it was Sunday. Kids had holiday in their playschool and Anjali had her day off in the hospital. She thought to visit Shreya in the evening. Yawning she woke up and went to take a bath. After shower, she made breakfast first and then woke up the twins. After the breakfast, she cleaned her house and was reading book and twins were playing with their toys when the doorbell rang. She wondered who would be at this afternoon as the kid's nanny was having her day off and she was not expecting any visitor today.

Sighing she stood up and went to open the door. Karan was impatiently waiting for Anjali to open the door. His breath got caught in his lungs when he saw her. She still looked so beautiful but her body had curves now. Giving birth definitely suited her.

Anjali froze seeing Karan on her door. How come he be here? How did he know about her and most importantly did he come to know about kids and has come to take them? These all thoughts were running a marathon in her head when she heard his voice "Long time no see Mrs.Oberoi" She came out of her reverie and frowned hearing him "Why are you here Karan? What do you want?"

Karan grinned at her and asked"Can't I come to meet my family darling? I missed you so much!!!" He tried to hug her to which Anjali squirmmed and took a step back. Annoyed she replied "Don't call me that and I don't remember asking you to come and meet me so you can leave now"2

Karan teased her "Trying to get rid of me? Believe me I won't let you do that this time and since you don't like darling how about sweetheart? I think it suits you well" Anjali glared at him and tried to close the door but he inserted his foot in between the doorway.

She scwoled at him and asked him to leave but he just ignored her and pushed her aside gently to enter her house. She ran after him to stop him but he just entered the house as if he owns it. She was constantly looking towards children's room that they won't come out.

"You got a nice home honey" Karan said to Anjali in a flirting manner after looking around the condo. She glared at him and said "I said don't call me that and you are not welcome here so leave and don't come back" He just whined "You are no fun wifey. We are meeting after four long years and you are not at all welcoming. Very bad and regarding leaving, let me burst your bubble that I am not leaving without you and our kids. Talking about them, I am dying to meet my children. Where are they?"1

Colour drained from Anjali's face on hearing him. So he not only knew about her whereabouts but he also knows about the twins. She shuttered "Wh... Which kids. I.. I do...don't have kids. Now leave please"

Easiness on his face went and he clenched his jaw "Don't you remember our kids Anjali. Those kids who stays with you and you have kept them apart from me for these all years. Where are my kids?"

Hearing the talking outside, twins decided to make their entry "Who is there mommy?" "Come and play with us mommy" both said to Anjali. Karan was shell shocked seeing his children for the first time. He couldn't believe that he and Anjali made the little miracles.

Seeing a stranger both hid behind their mother's legs and then peeped out "Who is he mommy?" Aarav asked his mother whereas Kiara just stared at him.Karan finally came out of his shock and glared at Anjali "Will you do the honour of introducing me to them or shall I do?" He dared her to deny him. She gulped and replied "Munchkins he is your..... yours" she couldn't understand how to tell them that he is their father. Karan continued on her behalf "Hello babies I am your father"

Both the children were surprised seeing their father. They both looked at Anjali for confirmation. Karan too challenged her to disagree. Sighing she faced the twins and said "Yes kiddos you both wanted to meet your daddy right! He is your daddy."

Both the kids left her leg and ran towards Karan. He scooped down to their levels and opened his arms for them. All three tightly hugged each other. Karan felt the happiest person in the world having his children in his arms. What could he not give up for this he thought. Aarav asked first "Where were you daddy? Why you didn't come to meet us?" Kiara then asked "Yes daddy mommy told you were busy with work so can't come to meet us but we missed you daddy"

Karan glared at Anjali hearing his kids whereas she had a guilty look on her face. He tightened his hold on them and replied "Daddy finished his work and came to live with you both now. Daddy too missed you darlings." Both the kids jumped hearing him "Really daddy now you will live with us. Me, Kiara, mommy and you?" Aarav asked hopefully. Kiara too requested him to stay with them. When he nodded his head they both clapped their hands with Glee.

He lifted both of them in his arms and went to sit on sofa with them sitting on their lap. Anjali was silently sitting in the corner watching the union of their kids with Karan. She was really surprised seeing him talking lovingly with them. He was patiently listening to them both. It was as if they had known each other since a long time. Seeing the happiness on all of their faces she felt guilty for keeping the twins away from their father. She may not allow Karan to be a part of her life but she won't stop him to be a part of their kids life.

After some time, it was twins lunch time so Anjali stood up and went near them "Come munchkins it's your lunch time" Aarav and Kiara both whined and told no as they didn't want to leave their Dad. Karan butted in between "Kids listen to your mommy and have your lunch. I will play with you two after you eat OK?" "really daddy" asked Kiara hopefully. He lifted her and Aarav in his arms and indicated Anjali to take him to dinning table. He made them both sit on their chairs and replied "yes now eat your lunch"

He was listening to the twins chatter and watching them eat when Anjali placed a plate of food in front of him. He raised an eyebrow in confusion when she told "Kids will like if you have lunch with them" She sat on the opposite chair and even though she could feel his eyes on her, she ignored him and continued to eat. After lunch, twins showed Karan the entire house and made him play with them. He picked up both of them and placed them on their bed when both fell asleep playing. Kissing their foreheads, he went out of their room to the living room where Anjali was reading book.

"We need to talk" he said her. Anjali kept her book on the coffee table and took a deep breath before looking at him "You can come and meet the kids any time you wish. Other than that, I am not interested in any talks" Karan scowled and sat on the sofa opposite to her and said "Anjali you can't ignore me you know that. Regarding the kids, I missed three years of their life thanks to you! I won't miss a single moment of their lives now so it would be better if you come back with me" She frowned hearing him and snapped at him "really Karan, are you for real? As far as I remember, you yourself distanced yourself from me four years back and asked me to maintain my distance from you. You blamed for the thing which I didn't do at all. Because of your indifference, I was forced to leave my family and go away and now you have the audacity to come back in my life again and ask me to go with you"1

Karan sighed and said "I know it was my mistake accusing you and distancing myself from you but believe me I couldn't make myself stop from falling for you. The first time I saw you, I knew I was in deep shit. You stirred the strong feelings in me and how much I tried to ignore them, I cannot do that. I realised that how much I try, I cannot help but fall in love with you and I can't live without you. The day I came back from Australia, I have decided to apologize to you for my behavior and confess my feelings for you but you had gone by then. I was trying to find you since last four years but you just disappeared like thin air. Please Anjali give me a chance to correct my mistakes and win you back. These few years without you were hell. Vidhya was my past but you are my present and future. I don't want to live without you and kids anymore. Even our families also miss you very much and eagerly waiting for you all back"

Tears welled up in her eyes. She sniffed and said "You are four years late Karan. I have learnt to live without you and our family and you all also just lived fine without me so leave me the hell alone. I don't want to go back. We can arrange visitation schedule for our children after the divorce"

Karan gasped hearing her and shouted "I won't divorce you. Not now not ever and I want to be a full time father to our kids so choice is yours. You can either come and live with us or live away from them because I won't live without them now" She glared at him "You cannot decide for me and I won't allow you to take them away from me. They are my life and dare you try to separate us"

Karan smirked at her "Believe me sweetheart, I too don't have any intention to take them away from you but you don't leave a choice for me. You know I can easily gain their full time custody if required" He knew kids were Anjali's weakness so she won't let him take them away from her. She would come back to him for their sake. It's just a matter of time for him to convince her and win her back. "Tell our kids that I will be back tomorrow morning. I hope to hear a positive answer from you. Bye honey, Love you" he said to her and pecked her cheeks and left. Anjali was shocked hearing him saying Love you. She too loved him but was afraid to trust him again.

CHAPTER THIRTY-FIVE

Kids spend the next entire day with their father. After putting kids to sleep, Anjali went in her room to sleep when her phone vibrated. She saw it was twin's nanny's message that she was sick and won't be able to come for few days. She got worried that who will look after her children now. Kids are having one week holiday as painting work is going on in their preschool and she won't be able to get leave from hospital except weekend. Even Shreya's house was on the other side of the town and moreover she was pregnant now. Looking after two small kids for full day would be difficult for her. She was having many friends but then twins was habitual to live with her and Shreya only.

Her phone rang when she was thinking of managing options for the kids. Seeing unknown number calling at night, she thought it would be of some patient. Hurriedly she picked up the phone "Hello Dr. Anjali Malhotra speaking" "Oh no my love, it's Dr. Anjali Oberoi darling. Don't you know that a girl's last name after marriage is her husband's last name. So it's Dr. Anjali Karan Oberoi" Karan said from the other side. She frowned hearing him and wondered how he got her number but then she thought that if he can manage to find her then getting her number is just a piece of cake for him. She kept her voice straight and asked "Why are you calling me now Karan? What do you want?"

Karan replied "I wanted to hear your voice darling so I called. Did the kids slept?" Anjali scwoled hearing him and said "Both the kids were tired after you left so they slept early and I remember telling not to try talking to me. I don't want to talk to you understood so don't call me" Karan ignored her words and teased her further "Ohh baby how I missed our small fights these past years. It's fun to see you getting mad and shouting my wild cat" She shouted "I am not your wild cat" He laughed hearing her.

"When can I meet the children tomorrow?" he asked Anjali. He doesn't need her permission to meet his kids but she was mad at him and he doesn't want to rile her up further so decided to give her some time to think. till then he will do any thing to please her. She replied "They are having holiday for one week as their preschool is undergoing painting so come home any time you wish. If you want to take them somewhere outside then give me address. I will drop them and pick them back from your hotel after my work" Karan thought for a while and said "No it's fine I will just come home to meet them and if they want to go out then I will take them and drop them back. You don't need to bother. Who look after the kids when you are at hospital?" Anjali replied "First my friend Shreya used to look after them when I am at the hospital but she got married last year and went to live with her husband on the other side of town so they have a nanny now. She is very reliable and takes care of them in my absence. But she just informed me now that she is sick and won't be able to come for a few days" Karan took this as an opportunity to spend more time with the kids and be close to anjali this way if he looks after them in her absence. He hopefully asked "Can I look after them when your are at the hospital. This way I will get to spend everyday with them and you don't have to worry about them" Anjali thought for a while. Both the kids became so fond of him when they met him for the first time and were even wanting to meet their daddy again so this way all three will get to spend time together and know each other. Moreover she won't be worried if the kids are with Karan. She took a deep breath and said "Ok come tomorrow morning before 9 AM. I need to leave for hospital by then. Good night" She disconnected the call saying that without giving him a chance to speak. Karan knew it would be difficult to gain her forgiveness but this opportunity will surely help him not only in bonding with his kids but also spend time with her.

CHAPTER THIRTY-SIX

Kids were spending time with their father and their bond with each other was getting stronger everyday. Karan did everything they asked and fulfilled their every wish. Anjali came back from work one evening when all three were watching TV. She greeted both the kids by kissing their cheeks and asking them about their day "How was your day kiddos? Had fun with Daddy?" Both the kids nodded excitedly. Kiara sequeled "Daddy bought us toys today mommy" Anjali didn't like Karan buying them whatever they wished at any time but she just smiled and didn't say anything because he was not in twins life earlier so he is fulfilling his longing by buying them whatever they want and allowing them to do whatever they like.

Karan was waiting for their greetings to get over. Then he said "Darlings tell your mommy to give daddy a kiss like you two" Aarav told Anjali "Mommy daddy is asking you to kiss him" She glared at Karan and said "Small kids only get kiss so tell your daddy NO" Kiara faced Karan "Mommy said no daddy" Karan pouted and kissed Anjali all of sudden on her cheek and said "Kids now ask mommy to return daddy's kiss. It's her turn now" Kiara hopefully asked her mother "Mommy please return daddy's kiss or he will feel bad. Please" She sighed and went near Karan to give him a small peck on his cheek but he suddenly turned his head and pecked her on her lips. She scwoled at him whereas he just grinned stupidly at the kids thanking them.

After dinner both the kids slept when Anjali went towards her room. Karan held her wrist and stopped her and said "It's been a week Anjali but you have still not spoken anything to me apart from talking about the kids. Please talk to me. Hit me, yell at me but say something dammit! I am tired of your silent treatment. Whenever I try to talk to you, you just avoid me like a plague. Please give me a chance to make up for my past mistakes" She removed her hand from his grip and said "If a person is not speaking with you then you should understand that he is not interested in talking with you and I even told you that I don't want to get involved with you again so why are you hell bent on getting close to me?"

Karan sighed and replied "I know you are angry with me but please forgive me at least for our children's sake. They won't be happy seeing us fighting" She frowned at him and answered " I am tolerating your presence in my life because of them so don't expect anything more from me. Now leave" He clenched his fists and pulled her towards him "Listen and listen carefully that I won't be going away from you three now and expect me to be an essential part of your life like our children. I love you and I will make you mine again within no time" Saying this, he smashed his lips on her. Anjali gasped at this and he took this opportunity to plunge his tongue in her mouth. She gained her senses after few seconds and pushed him but he pulled her further into him. She gave up after a few seconds and kissed him back. Both of them were kissing each other madly and pouring out their love and longing of last four years in their kiss.

Karan parted from her lips and started kissing her jawline. Anjali fisted his hair and moaned. Karan breathlessly asked her "Do you want to continue this Anjali? There will be no going back from this" Anjali's mind was clouded with passion. She knew what they were doing was not right but she couldn't control herself . She desperately wanted to be loved by Karan so she just kissed him. He took this as her indication and lifted her up in his arms without breaking the kiss and went in her room. They both spend their entire night showing how much they missed each other.

It was early in the morning when Anjali was sleeping in Karan's arm. She thought can't she forgive him and give their relationship a second chance. Every person makes mistake but she was afraid that her heart won't be able to bear the pain again if Karan goes back to his old self. She decided to take warm shower and clear her mind when a pair of hands pulled her back to bed. Karan was looking at her and saw the confusion on her face. He asked "What happened sweetheart? You are not regretting what happened between us last night right?" She sighed and sat on the bed resting her head on the backrest "No I am not regretting about what happened between us. It's just that I forgave you Karan but I cannot trust you. I know everyone deserves a second chance and so do you but I am afraid that if you will get back to you old aloofness side then I won't be able to bear the rejection second time"1

Karan too sat up and pulled her in his lap and kissed her on forehead "Baby I know I was wrong in treating you indifferently but believe me I have changed. You and our kids are my life now. I won't ever give you or our children any chance of complain. Just trust me honey. When I said I love you, I truly mean it. I realized it late but you are my true Soulmate. I will always be yours. Vidhya was my past but you are my present and future. You came and pulled me from the darkness and filled my life with colours, gave me two wonderful kids. Let me take away all your pain and fill your life with happiness please"

Tears flowed from her eyes and she hugged him tight. She sniffed and said "I love you too Karan. I missed you so much" Karan tightened his embrace hearing her and kissed her hard.

He said "Our families are waiting for you and kids eagerly. Let's go back to our home darling" She gave him a watery smile and nodded her head in agreement.

Anjali came back from hospital when she saw her house was in darkness. She frowned and thought that where were everyone. Wondering that she went to switch on the light when suddenly lights filled the whole room and she saw all her family members standing and singing Happy Birthday song for her. Karan was holding a cake with a smile on his face.

After cutting the cake and chatting with their families, they both put the kids to sleep. Anjali came out from the washroom after freshing up when Karan hugged her from behind and kissed her on the neck "Happy birthday love. Did you like the surprise?" Anjali smiled and rested her back on his chest " Thank you so much for a surprise party honey. It's been so long since we spend time with both our families. I really enjoyed today. With Pakhi being pregnant earlier and mom and dad living with her and Arjun to take care of mother and new baby, its been a while we meet them. Baby Ahana had grown so much since we saw her last. Even I asked my Papa and Mumma to go on a world tour. He is still working like teenager instead of retiring"

Karan bite her on her shoulder and said "I want my return gift darling" Anjali became confused and asked "What do you want Karan?" He continued kissing her and replied "Why don't I show you what I want rather than telling" With this he lifted her and carried her towards their bed. Anjali giggled at him and said "Oh God honey we are married since last eight years and you are father of two seven year old kids still you are too flirt" He just ignored her and continued to worship her body.

After their wonderful lovemaking, they both were wrapped in a blanket and cuddling when Anjali said "Time flies so fast Karan. I thought I will never see you again after I left you but God gave us a second chance and we are happily together now" Karan nodded and replied "Yes darling God brought us together again because you are my Soulmate. I love you" She too kissed him and replied "I love you too baby" Karan grinned hearing her and both of them slept holding each other.